MW00608641

Adventures of a Traveling Dog Salesman

Return to Alaska

By Matt Snader

Forward by Josh Snader

Published by Alaska Land Barons, LLC

Anchor Point, Alaska

www.AlaskaLandBarons.com

ISBN 978-1-4951-6940-3

51399>

9 781495 169403

Table of Contents

Blog Entries included throughout the book:

- "The Limo" rides again!
- Limo blows a tire, attempts homicide, a guy named Paul comes to the rescue
- Cabin construction begins, concerned neighbor offers to loan guns
- Moosetracks: Not just an ice cream flavor
- The bare essentials, don't play capture the flag in our woods
- Enthusiasm reigns over new throne, Maiden flush proves successful
- Limo gets stuck in bank drive through, causes small traffic jam
- Van selects "Benedict Arnold" as role model, Suburban is old reliable
- Trailer blows last tire, collapses and joins the van club
- Suburban breaks down within walking distance of cheap van for sale
- "The Grid" is officially a dinosaur (and an expensive one)

This book is true, written in mostly chronological order. You may notice that some of the blog posts reference events are slightly out of order in the book. While it is quite doubtful the historical accuracy of this book will ever be of any significance, we have done the best we can to present everything factually and straightforward. As hard as this may be to believe, all details about Matt's ancestors are accurate. It is flattering (I think) that some folks thought our blog entries were fictional because "they couldn't possibly be true". I assure you they are.

Also in this book we outline some of our personal background that laid the foundation for the events that take place in this book. Part of this is our faith in God, and we have included several occasions that were instrumental in shaping this part of our life. It is our belief that anyone who reads the Bible and believes it, with simple faith, can and will have prayers answered (although God should not be viewed as Santa Claus). The most exciting answer to prayer: For whosoever shall call upon the name of the Lord shall be saved. Romans 10:13

We have also included material that may not be directly related, but supplemental, such as Josh's blog post on the local Alaska coffee shop we frequent, etc. Hopefully you do not find this content confusing and disruptive to the flow of the book. I have been accused of having ADHD in the past.

To be sensitive to British readers, we may not have all punctuation inside quotation marks. We also extend this sensitivity to those who may struggle with grammar...

Don't miss the experience that started it all!

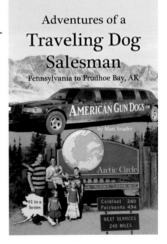

In 2013 our family drove to Alaska from Pennsylvania. The rest is history!

80 Pages, full color. Suggested retail $9.95 Available at book stores and online at www.AlaskaLandBarons.com

Next Book Title:

Book 3: Year of Much Fishing

We had already been in Alaska for two summers-but had not yet really went Halibut fishing, or went for a boat ride. This terrible situation was corrected in the summer of 2015, with dividends. Also ride along as we go gold panning above Fairbanks, try our hand at homesteading, and hunt wild pigs in Florida. Also included is the saga of how Matt won an ebay auction for a 27' boat and hauled it 4,000+ miles to Alaska (boats are cheaper in Pa).

3

Meet the Snader family! Above: Matt & Marlene Snader

Below left to right: Samantha, Kallia, Desiree, Mary Kate, Shane, Lana

The Snader family currently resides in Anchor Point, Alaska. They enjoy the great outdoors and all that Alaska has to offer.

Our special thanks to these businesses that help make our story possible:

Sterling Supply LLC

Located in Sterling, Alaska. A great place to find your next storage shed, barn or cabin!

33350 Sterling Hwy, Sterling, Alaska
Phone (907) 953-4402

Frontier Ice & Bakery

Located on the outskirts of Soldotna, Alaska. A great place to find ice and baked goods.

(907) 841-8718

Stupend.us!

The website that caused an online uproar with a spoof news article "PA bans NJ drivers". Operated by my brother, Josh Snader. Josh helped me write this book and build the cabin. The website again is: www.stupend.us.

John 3:16 & 17 For God so loved the world, that he gave his only begotten Son, that whosoever believeth in him should not perish, but have everlasting life. For God sent not his Son into the world to condemn the world; but that the world through him might be saved.

Rissler Garage Doors
Rissler Garage Doors

171 Napierville Road,
Ephrata, PA 17522
Phone: 717-738-DOOR
Fax: 717-738-0926

www.RisslerDoor.com

Garage Door Service, Sales and Installation

Clark Hill Service Center

570-539-8878—Mt Pleasant Mills, Pennsylvania

This is where most of the limo work was carried out, and the 27 foot Ebay boat that is in the next book. Arlan also does PA state inspections (something not required in Alaska) and vehicle repairs, tires, oil changes, etc. He normally does not paint vehicles, but might if you beg him enough. Thanks Arlan for all your help! A special thanks is due because, well just read the book and you will see.

A very special thanks to:

Alan & Twila Reinford and family

Marlin & Karen Eicher and family

Luis & Shelly Yoder

Harlan & Carolyn Rissler

The staff at Online Advertising, LLC for putting up with my running off to Alaska

My brother Josh

And my parents, for taking their first airplane ride to come visit us.

In his hand *are* the deep places of the earth: the strength of the hills *is* his also. Psalms 95:4

U.S. Bureau of Consular Affairs Issues Travel Advisory for the State of Alaska

The U.S. Bureau of Consular Affairs issued a travel advisory for the state of Alaska warning that the state of Alaska has been known to cause mental illness, short term memory loss, and even a loss of a personal sense of hygiene. Officials have cited numerous incidents of travelers never returning from the far north state in the same state of mind, or in some cases, never returning at all, as a basis for the advisory.

The advisory stems from the dozens of documented reports of returning Alaskan tourists being taken to doctors by their families because of their family's suspicion that they have developed mental health issues. Clarence Williams was affected by 'Post-Alaska Depression (or PAD) when her brother returned from Alaska and started exhibiting signs of mental distress. "It was unnerving," she says, "when we met him at the airport to pick him up he looked like a wild man since he hadn't shaved since he left." She says he's also looking for real estate in Alaska despite the family's pleas to get back into the routine of his former mundane, everyday life. "He used to be so predictable. Something snapped. Something's changed. I don't like it. What would possess someone to grow a beard and buy land 4,500 miles away in the middle of nowhere? It's just not natural."

Officials warn that traveling to Alaska can also incite altercations with the tourist's home towns and communities. Several municipalities in Pennsylvania reported a significant rise in the amount of neighborhood disturbances instigated by people who recently returned from Alaska. Richard Martin is on the Lancaster County zoning board. He says people struggling from Post Alaska Depression cause a number of problems. "We've had people come back [from Alaska] and set up gun ranges in their backyards which disturbs and offends sensible folks. We had a guy try to start raising moose in his 2 acre suburban plot because he thought the neighborhood was too 'boring.' Another guy started raising a 16 dog sled team in the middle of a development which, as you can imagine, caused a little bit of anger among the neighbors. This other guy actually bought a float plane, put it in his tiny backyard pond, and insisted on living in it. It didn't meet our building codes so we made the dumb guy get rid of it." Martin shook his head. "The wanna be Alaskans are troublesome and they refuse to assimilate into civilized culture." Martin said a common way to spot someone who has PAD, or is likely to travel to Alaska, is a strong and vocal dislike of overreaching government regulations. "It's important to keep people who are already troublesome and pushing against local regulations away from Alaska because once they get that taste of unbridled freedom they are always resistant to the zoning board and our expansive collection of laws. We're just trying to make their lives easier by telling them exactly what to do with their lives and money."

The Bureau of Consular Affairs, which is in charge of issuing travel advisories at home and abroad, released an educational pamphlet in conjunction with the advisory which was aimed at raising awareness of Post Alaska Depression and the steps which are to be taken to avoid it:

Symptoms *of the condition may include a yearning to visit Alaska again, even immediately after returning. The victim may also display an irrational desire to be in the company of large dangerous game, such as grizzly bears and moose, that are native to the state of Alaska. Victims have been known to shun razors and refer to themselves as "Alaskan bushmen" which is categorically false because they aren't living in Alaska and couldn't survive two days in the type of terrain referred to as "bush." These delusions are typically from the dementia and/or short term memory loss that comes with Post Alaska Depression (PAD). Other more minor symptoms include a sudden spike in Alaska related activities such as (1) Reading informational articles on Wikipedia about Alaska which no sane person would voluntarily read under any other circumstances, (2) expressing a desire to raise a sled dog team or construct a home made sled for a sled dog team, (3) build a log cabin with only an ax, (4) staring at pictures or screen savers of Alaska – or any mountains, wildlife, or weather found in the state – in a lifeless, listless, catatonic manner with a refusal to be cheered (5) or tote a large handgun on their person everywhere they go despite local laws specifically prohibiting that behavior.*

*Tragically, as of the time of publication, **there is no known cure for PAD**. Once contracted, PAD can make victims suffer for years with the symptoms either fading to tolerable measures with occasional flare ups, or worsening until the victim moves to Alaska and is never heard from again.*

*The best measure is prevention. Remember, an ounce of prevention is worth a pound of cure. **That's why, as of June 2, 2014, we are issuing a travel advisory against the state of Alaska.***

Note: This article is a satire post Josh put on his blog. However I thought perhaps it might have a ring of truth to it.

"We are all Going to die"

Chapter 1

Where: 25,000 feet over Mount Redoubt, Alaska

When: December 15, 1989

So far it had been routine flight for KLM Flight 867, piloted by Captain Karl van der Elst. The Boeing 747 had taken off from Amsterdam and was on route to Tokyo, with a layover in Anchorage International Airport. Mount Redoubt had erupted the day before, and traffic control was keeping an eye on it. Unknown to air traffic control, however, was the fact the ash plume had no moisture content. This made it invisible to radar. Flight 867 flew directly into it, and all 4 engines immediately clogged up with ash, triggered the overheat sensors, and shut off.

The following transmissions took place between Anchorage Center, the air traffic control facility for that region, and KLM 867:

Pilot — "KLM 867 heavy is reaching level 250 heading 140"

Anchorage Center— "Okay, Do you have good sight on the ash plume at this time?"

Pilot — "Yea, it's just cloudy it could be ashes. It's just a little browner than the normal cloud."

Pilot — "We have to go left now. . . it's smoky in the cockpit at the moment, sir."

Anchorage Center— "KLM 867 heavy, roger, left at your discretion."

Pilot — "Climbing to level 390, we're in a black cloud, heading 130."

Pilot — "KLM 867 we have flame out all engines and we are descending now!"

Anchorage Center— "KLM 867 heavy, Anchorage?

Pilot — "KLM 867 heavy, we are descending now. . . we are in a fall!"

Pilot — "KLM 867, we need all the assistance you have, sir. Give us radar vectors please!"

Radar vectors give the plane more room to navigate, something that is not a luxury when your 747's four engines all go dead at once. At this point, Flight 867 had two options: 1. Crash into mountains. 2. Crash into the ocean. The pilot and crew were not fond of these limited options, so they worked furiously to get the engines restarted. One passenger onboard reported "It felt like the nose of the plane had a huge weight on it, and we were dropping fast." They also mentioned there was "near panic" in the passengers. This panic was reportedly not helped by the captain telling passengers "We are all going to die."

The disabled plane dropped over 14,000 feet in only a few minutes of time. Passengers were writing their last wishes and goodbyes to friends and family on various articles. The pilot wondered how landing the 747 in the inlet might go. At that point no one had ever crash landed a 747 into an ocean and lived to tell about it. He must have felt it was a bad idea, as he and crew repeatedly tried restarting the stalled engines.

Finally, the engines all started. One engine kept flaming out, but three engines were enough to limp to Anchorage. The passengers were transferred to another plane and continued on to Tokyo. The plane was only 6 months old when the incident occurred, but all 4 engines needed to be replaced before it flew again. The engines were replaced, the complete repairs came with a price tag of $80 million. That is cheaper than buying a new plane, I guess. The aircraft involved was still in service, as of 2008. The captain and crew were hailed as heroes, I'm sure.

So what does this story have to do with me? Nothing, really. I was only 7 years old at the time, and firmly planted on the ground in Pennsylvania. However, Mount Redoubt can be seen out the front of our cabin windows in our land in Alaska. Cook Inlet is 4 miles down the road. At least part of this incident (if nothing else the problem causing ash cloud spewing from the volcano) would have been visible from an observer standing on my land in Alaska, and I can't help but think that is intriguing.

Mount Redoubt is still an active volcano, the last major eruption was in 2009. Although we have seen it puff a few times. We are at least 50 miles from Redoubt, so it's very doubtful it will ever kill us. The 2009 eruption inconvenienced the neighbors. It still causes some issues, such as dulling your chainsaw quickly when cutting firewood. The ash is very abrasive. When the volcanic ash is in the air you need to take special measures to protect your engine, as the ash is fine enough to go through a regular air filter.

Picture of the 1989 eruption of Mount Redoubt. Photo courtesy of Wikipedia. Photo taken by PD-USGOV-INTERIOR-USGS

Life in the Lower 48
Chapter 2

Alaska. Just the name sends a burst of adrenaline through my system. Had Josh's article not been a satire post, I would have assumed I came down hard with "Post-Alaska Depression." The good news is that the desire to return to Alaska is not actually a mental illness. After our return from our Alaska road trip in 2013, I had a burning desire to return. In fact, that desire burned stronger and stronger, until we again packed up the limo and left Pennsylvania. Here is our story.

We arrived back from Alaska in early July of 2013. It was nice to be home, as living on the road gets tiresome, even in a 28 foot long stretch limo. I even remember thinking "it's good to be back." Remarkably, I even told some people that I like "Snyder County better than Alaska." These feelings, however, were temporary and insane. Some experts, who I expect are crazy, claim that a butterfly can cause a hurricane. Simply put, a small disturbance at just the right time and place can alter complete weather patterns. The disturbance caused by visiting Alaska should be compared to crashing a B52 full of nukes into the Grand Canyon, instead of butterfly wings (On a side note scientists are developing combat gear with Nano particles based on the butterfly wing).

Consider the situation that caused us to move out to Snyder County, from Lancaster County. Marlene and I had considered moving out of Lancaster County, simply because of all the people. Our house was 30 feet off of route 23, which made the problem much worse. Some days it would take 5 minutes of waiting for a break in traffic to exit our driveway. Marlene and I both agree that we would like a more rural area better. Having not yet toured Alaska, we simply assumed central Pa was "rural." Our biggest obstacle to moving was the small fact we were completely broke.

Buying land without money can be a challenge, and after looking at various properties in Snyder County, we simply gave up. So we continued to live beside route 23, with hordes of people living in every direction around us. One day a small event happened that caused a complete change in our lives. Marlene was in the house, and she heard a "whack, whack, whack" outside. Looking out the window, she noticed the neighbor boy beating on concrete attached to our house. She walked outside and asked this fellow why he was destroying our property. He flatly denied he had done such a thing, and walked off. This was not the first run in with the neighbors. One time their Rottweiler attempted to attack me in my own driveway, and I informed them (my adrenaline was running very high at the moment) in no uncertain, undiplomatic terms that their dog was running a high risk of getting shot. Another time the neighbor children took the liberty of spray painting their names on our trees (later on our own children also spray painted our trees, it must be a part of growing up). Our Mustang also got "custom" paint. And so on. If you attempted to talk to the neighbor lady, and whatever man happened to be living with her at the moment, they would "chew" you out for being so insensitive.

Marlene was not very happy about being blatantly lied to by our belligerent neighbors. Inspired, she went inside, and started looking, again, at property in central Pa. She found a small 3 bedroom house on 2 acres in Snyder County, PA for $78,000. Remarkably, arrangements for buying this house fell into place, and we moved. The point of the story is, had the neighbor boy not vandalized our house in Lancaster County we may still be living there. I also need to note that our house in Lancaster had been a blessing, and it filled a need when we bought it. A realtor named Kurt Paddock bent over backwards to help us purchase our house in Lancaster County several years prior, and I am thankful for his efforts. I consider him a personal friend. However that chapter in our lives had closed, and it was time for our next step. I don't hate Lancaster County-it's just too crowded for my tastes.

The verse Romans 8:28 comes to mind "And we know that all things work together for good to them that love God, to them who are the called according to His purpose." I firmly believe this verse is true, and have seen evidence of it many times. One example is attacks by extreme animal rights activists on our websites. We have several websites for pet classifieds, the most well known is LancasterPuppies.com. Activists would post all kinds of hateful things online about our website, most of which were blatantly false and patently absurd. Crazy things like saying breeders raise beagles in dishwashers, ram pipes down dogs throats to keep them from barking, etc. (these practices are also very illegal) In the event someone actually did something in poor judgment, it was portrayed as the norm for all kennels. Many of the claims were so outrageous anyone with sense could see they were false. Ironically all these posts raised our search engine rankings, resulting in more sales and higher web traffic.

Answer to Prayer-or a coincidence?

I am a Christian. I have seen prayers answered many times, but skeptics will often point out that they could be coincidences. Let me share this true, unembellished experience I had.

After moving to Snyder County, we rented our old house in Lancaster out. This arrangement worked out good for a year or two, but I tired of keeping after the maintenance of a second house, so I decided to sell it. I told the renters they had to move out. It took them a month or two to find another house, but they did, and moved. Then I tried to sell our old house. Several months went by, and it didn't sell. So here I was, paying two mortgages, two sets of property taxes, etc.

Snyder County is a 2 hour drive from Lancaster, give or take a few minutes. I was not at our old property much, but one day I was in the basement, fixing a few odds and ends, hoping it would help the house sell better. I had decided to list it with a realtor, and the realtor had given me a list of things he wanted fixed before he would list it. Mostly cosmetic things, but time consuming and costly. I was also worried about just being able to keep paying the mortgage without a rent check coming in.

I stood in the cellar stairwell, feeling a bit overwhelmed. So I prayed "God, please send me a clear sign what I should do with this place, something so clear even some one as dull as me understands it." It was just a quick, simple prayer, but very sincere.

I think it was less than 10 minutes later, but it could have been as much as 15 minutes, I heard a knock on the back door. There stood the lady who used to rent our house! "Hello, can I help you?" I asked. "Yes", she replied. "We were wondering if we could rent your house again".

They moved in before the week was over!

(and the realtors to do list went in the trash)

I don't think this was a coincidence.

Back to our Alaska dilemma. Here we were, living in Snyder County. Not a bad place to live by any decent person's standards, however Alaska had captivated our hearts. Actually, it wasn't just Alaska. Marlene and I discussed various other states, such as Texas, Wyoming, Montana, North Dakota and South Dakota. You may be noticing a trend. The more rural, the more attractive. If it happened to have low taxes, even better. Then Alaska played the trump card: No taxes, and they pay you to live there! And then Snyder County struck a blow.

Marlene was actually the one that insisted on Alaska. She said "If we move, we might as well do it right." Sound advice. In fact it turned out to be the equivalent of throwing gasoline on a fire. Before 12 months had passed, we were card carrying Alaskans. (flex) (A little Skype lingo there) So here is our story, in mostly chronological order.

In the late summer of 2013, about 6 weeks after returning from Alaska, an event occurred which made me extremely dissatisfied with our property in Middleburg, Pa. Up until this point I was very satisfied with it. The occasion was our company picnic. I like to think our company picnics are the best around.

No decent company picnic is complete without guns and explosions. A strange (according to some) work picnic tradition we developed was blowing up appliances. It started one year when a microwave gave out before the picnic, and we dispatched it with a 4 pound exploding target. Yes, exploding targets are legal. A 4 pound exploding target is the equivalent to 4 sticks of dynamite. Good stuff. As the name suggests, you shoot it with a high powered rifle to set it off. This is a built in safety feature, as most children don't use high powered rifles.

The appliance we selected for this occasion was an old electric heater. Stoutly built, from what I would have guessed the 1960 era. It was in our house when bought it. The heater worked fine, but when you plugged it in, the smell was like an overused outhouse at the end of a long, hot summer. Not being fond of the aroma, I decided it was time to retire the heater.

Blowing up the heater was uneventful. It did rip leaves and small branches off the trees around the detonation site, and drove pieces of metal into nearby tree trunks. Perhaps had we stopped there, we would have been ok. But you know how setting off exploding targets goes, one is not enough. So we set off several more. Then came the straw that broke the camels back. My brother in law, Paul, was there with a Rugar Mini 14, with a 30 round clip. I also had an AR-15 (they are legal for hunting in Alaska and Texas) with a 30 round clip. We decided to have a simple contest, and see who could empty their gun the quickest, in a safe direction (of course). I don't remember who won, but shortly thereafter someone said "hey your neighbor is here." Wanting to be neighborly, of course, I quickly walked over to him.

"Uh, your kinda making a lot of noise, and I think it's enough for today" or something like that, he said. He was very polite, and cordial. He went to great lengths to point out he supported firearms ownership, even calling attention to NRA stickers on his Jeep. Fortunately the next event on our company picnic schedule was the knife throwing contest, which didn't make much noise. However, something broke inside me. This was the first time (believe it or not) I had ever been told to stop shooting on my own property. No, I don't hold it against the neighbors. They were decent about it, but the problem was, I couldn't shoot now without worry that I was upsetting someone. The whole point of rural living had been compromised.

Our knife throwing contest is simple. I take various bills, from $1 to $50 and pin them on the targets. The larger bills are folded up, making them harder to hit. First person to stick a knife through the bill, gets to keep it. This turns our employees into very enthusiastic knife throwers. That day Ken took the top prize, a $50 bill.

A quick note on work picnics: Naturally some high strung folks will think guns, explosions, and knife throwing contests don't belong at work picnics. I ask why not? It's my company-if it's all legal and no one gets hurt, what does it matter? I should mention our work picnics never involved alcohol. If they did, I would certainly agree that our choice of festivities would not be appropriate.

I'm not a professional knife thrower, but I did actually throw these knives for the picture. I hate to admit it but it took me more than one try...

"The Limo" rides again!

Submitted on Wed, 11/13/2013

My last blog entry I reported the Limo was having some issues with blowing clouds of smoke and oil guzzling. Not wanting to disappoint humanity in general by scrapping it, (and of course Larry Burket recommends repairing your car rather than purchasing a new one. and have you seen the price of new limos lately?) We purchased a rebuilt long block 4.6 from a local auto parts store. They were so thrilled by my order they gave me a free bumper sticker and a Dr. Pepper. Ironically, the long built engine cost almost exactly the same price as I paid for the car itself (well over, if you consider all the extra parts I put on "while it was apart". Auto part shops are quite good at instilling fear of other parts failing).

Which leads me to another odd phenomenon, some folks when they see the Limo, are like "does that thing have a 460?". Only a few decimal points off, actually, it's a 4.6 V-8. Then they proceed to spout forth great words of amazement that a car that big would have an engine so small. Well, the car actually weighs less than a 4x4 F-150, and quite a few of them have 4.6's, some even have smaller V-6's. And I'm not really interested in installing a 460 cubic inch engine, as I bet my fuel mileage would be less than 22 mpg. (like 8 or 9) But I digress.

So after ordering this engine, the next item on the list is to remove the old one. Arlan from Clark Hill Service Center (located in Mt. Pleasant Mills, Pa, phone 570-539-8878) graciously allowed me to hog his largest bay in the garage for over a week while we hacked away at the project. I figured we'll yank the engine out one day, and install the new one the next. The last time I switched an engine was 15 years ago in a 1978 Ford Granada, and boy, have they made things more complex since then. The whole project took over a week, and would have taken a month, had it not been for Arlan's most appreciated help and advice.

Naturally, I didn't want to waste an opportunity, so I repainted the car while it was under Arlan's roof. I'll post some pictures of this new paint job soon. This also demonstrated Arlan's patience, he had to stagger through paint fumes and sanding dust while working in his other bays (although he drew the line about shooting paint while other cars were in the garage).

While I was in the midst of the project, customers would walk in the shop. Then it was common to see them talk to Arlan in hushed whispers, glancing backwards my way. Arlan hinted that they were discussing such issues as financial irresponsibility, insanity, and other life issues. I'm glad I could help Arlan connect closer with his customers.

Anyway, finally the time came to start it up. This momentous day was November 11, 2013. After hearing many horror stories of new engines exploding, throwing rods, and self destructing over small, seemingly insignificant mistakes, I expect it to blow the roof off the garage. The worst thing that happened was a heater hose disconnected, but I can deal with that. Much to my relief it kept running.

To test out the new engine, one of our employees, Leon (who is the manager of our Ohio office) and his wife Trista, volunteered to drive the limo to Georgia and back. So last night at 1am they rolled in to pickup the car. I haven't heard anything from them, so I am assuming it's performing flawlessly. I'll post trip updates from them as they come in. Also, if you happen to see the limo rolling down the highway, send us a picture for our "Limo Sightings" page.

The Limo Gets a Rebuild and a New Paint Job

Chapter 3

After we returned from Alaska, I experienced a string of annoying issues with the limo. The first issue to crop up was the starter. Several times I had to crawl under the car and beat the starter with a hammer to get it to turn over. That only lasted so long, and then the starter stopped for good. Thankfully, this was in my driveway, so I just replaced the starter right there.

The next problem was the engine. It started smoking very vigorously and taking oil at a frightening pace. I tried to ignore this phenomenon, as the car still ran fine. One day, Arlan, my mechanic, noticed this trend. "Your engine is shot" he told me. I told him I didn't care if it took oil, let it smoke. Arlan informed me that, sure, I could do that, but one day "it will go poof, probably at a bad spot." I'm not sure how he actually said it, but it was something like that.

I have had too many bad experiences with junk yard engines that I care to mention. So I priced some remanufactured engines, and ended up getting one from Advanced Auto parts. I suspect all these auto parts places get their engines from the rebuild company, because strangely, they all said they had a 4.6 V8 long block available, but it needed to be shipped up from Texas.

Another issue was the paint was fading and peeling. This paint job was only 6 months old, but I had used spray paint cans. Not really the best way to paint a car, but it had been an experiment. So I decided on a plan, we would paint the car and replace the engine in one sweep. Arlan graciously let me do this project in one of his garage bays. Had he known how involved and time consuming this was about to get, he may have chased me off before I had a chance to start. But he couldn't have been too uninformed, as this was the 4th or maybe 5th time I was painting a vehicle at his place (I have a soft spot in my heart for painting things).

When I picked up the new engine, I was told it had an unlimited mileage 3 year warranty. "So I can drive this back and forth all I want to say, Alaska?" I asked the clerk. She laughed, and said, "sure, no problem." Despite this fact, they wanted the odometer reading on the car. Not sure how this would help much, because the odometer doesn't work.

Arlan manhandles the engine, while his shop helper (I think his name was Ryan) attempts to pry something loose.

The new engine, ready to install.

The new engine installation went without a hitch, except taking longer than I expected (which is very normal). The painting process was a little painstaking, as each layer of the camouflage I had to tape off. We topped it off with a coat of clear coat, and then of course applied the new lettering on the side. This time we used "real" car paint.

On our test run, I discovered the turn signals did not work. Later, Arlan discovered I had run a dry wall screw into the side to hold the trim down, and it went through a wiring harness. Three days after we got the car back together, Leon from our office tested it out by driving it to Georgia to visit one of our customers. Leon is our office manager at our Ohio location. He made the 1,600 mile trip without turn signals.

Once Leon flipped his car (not the limo) on the roof. Being a practical man of character and thrift, he rolled the car back on the wheels, beat the roof back up with a sledgehammer and kept driving it. So driving around without turn signals in a 28 foot stretch limo was something he could manage.

Below is a picture of the Limo in Georgia on the maiden voyage of the new engine. Needless to say, the limo made the trip without incident. Leon's wife, Trista, who also works for us, is standing in front of the car.

Before running the Limo and trailer on a long trip such as to Alaska, we decided to take it on two more short test runs. First, I ran it down to Texas to help out a dog breeder setup his kennel. On the way we swung by this place that sells ducks calls and such, to see if they were interested in buying any hunting dogs. Unfortunately we couldn't locate the owners that day.

The trip to Texas turned out to be a rather horrid one. Almost everyone got sick (we had the whole family with) and with the exception of Marlene we all took turns throwing up in the car.

Upon our return, the Snyder County times ran an article about the trip. They left out the parts about the vomiting, and instead focused on my comments about eating at "Willy's Duck Diner." The highlight at the diner was eating local "Alligator tenders", which look and taste like chicken, only for twice as much money. We did enjoy the diner. Believe it or not, they also served duck.

American Gun Dogs Limo Heads To Duck Dynasty
By Kay Poeth

The American Gun Dogs limo parks in front of Willy's Duck Diner.

The American Gun Dogs limo took another road trip! After their trip to Alaska, the engine was replaced. The vehicle was repainted in camouflage, of course, and the windshield was replaced. On January 4, 2014, the Snader family traveled to South Monroe, LA to the "Duck Dynasty" headquarters.

It was a whirlwind trip covering 3,000 miles with a side trip to Texas on the way home. The Snaders returned home on January 11. Although the purpose of the trip was to meet with dog breeder in Georgia and Texas, the lure of "Duck Dynasty" was too strong to resist.

Matt Snader reported in his blog, "We stayed right in South Monroe at a motel, and I was startled to see a 'Willy's Duck Diner' across the parking lot. Sure enough, it's the same 'Willie' from 'Duck Dynasty.' Having watched 'Leave it to Beavers,' I thought 'the Beards' were not interested in restaurants. However, they must have gotten their act together since that episode as the food was very good. I even sampled some deep fried gator. I was hoping to hear some shouting and see 'ol Si making fireballs off the grill, but apparently he works another shift."

The Snaders also visited Duck Commander Headquarters. However, the Robertsons were not milling around the store signing autographs much to Matt's disappointment. However, Matt noted, "We got some curious glances around Duck Commander with the limo, but apparently camouflage limos are standard fare in that corner of town. No one acted very startled to see another one, anyway."

Note that our sickness had nothing to do with Willy's Duck Diner. (I would hate to get sued for defamation) The sickness occurred several days after our stop at the diner, so I'm quite sure the two events were unrelated.

We were also helping another dog breeder get setup, this time in Colorad. So Ken from our office, and his wife Kathleen, transported some supplies out to the new kennel. On this trip the Limo and trailer performed flawlessly, except for one bad omen, which I stupidly failed to heed. It was about 4,000 miles to Colorado and back. When Ken returned the Limo and trailer, the trailer tires were bald. "That's strange" I thought. But I figured we would just put new tires on before heading to Alaska, and purchase a second spare tire to take along (we had not taken the trailer to Texas).

Ken reported one humorous incident that occurred at a rest area. He was back checking the trailer, and a policeman walked up. Worried he was breaking a law he was unaware of, he asked the police if there was a problem. "Oh no, I just wanted to take a picture of your car!" the police replied. He then reported seeing it in the "Ducks Unlimited" magazine, and was glad to see it in person! Ken did admit to hitting speeds well above the suggested 55 mph limit for the little trailer tires, perhaps that explains his apprehension with talking to Colorado's finest.

Ken also said the "limo didn't have much power at high elevations." When I noticed the sign with the elevation marker, that suddenly made more

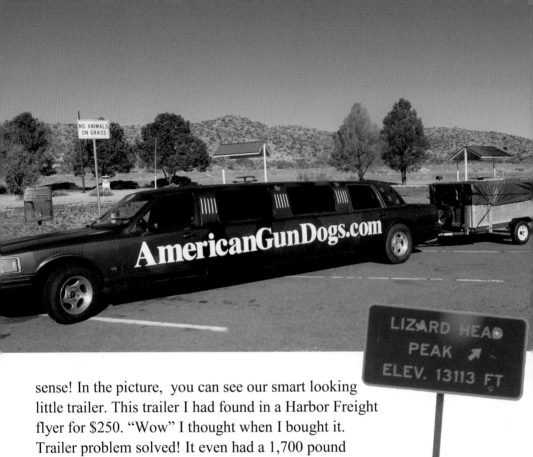

sense! In the picture, you can see our smart looking
little trailer. This trailer I had found in a Harbor Freight
flyer for $250. "Wow" I thought when I bought it.
Trailer problem solved! It even had a 1,700 pound
gross weight limit, according to the flyer.

The trailer needed some assembly, because it
came in a box. I had taken it to Clark Hill Service

Center and got Arlan to assemble it for me. My friend, Shannon High, is good at making sides for trailers, so I got him to put sides on it. We had a handsome little trailer, for around $800. Little did I realize this trailer would be a thorn in my side.

One day, I noticed the limo was wearing out the inside of the one front tire. I called around and finally found a garage with a machine to accommodate the car. Because of it's length, it did not fit on all alignment racks. I told Hank*, at Dumpy Hank's Garage*, that all I wanted was an alignment. "Ok, sure" he said. So I dropped the car off, and hoped for the best. The next day Hank called, with a serious tone in his voice. "Your car is dangerous to drive" he said. "The ball joints are about ready to fall out." I decided Hank must be one of those con artist mechanics, after all I noticed a "financing available" sign in his garage.

Not wanting to tell Hank I thought he was a weasel, or maybe an overzealous perfectionist, I politely declined a laundry list of suggested repairs (which amounted to $1,500+) and picked the limo up. Some of the parts he had suggested replacing because "they looked worn." Had I told Hank what I thought, I was afraid he would have dumped sugar in my gas or thrown a dead rat under the seat, although Hank didn't really seem like that type of person. Since Hank's grave diagnostic, I have driven the limo over 10,000 miles on some of the roughest roads in North America. Although Hank may have been right, as a year later we did spend quite a bit of money on the limo's front suspension.   *Not real name

The only time your dog would need to be licensed in Alaska

Answer to Prayer-or a coincidence?

In 2007 we decided to expand our dog advertising operation to Ohio. We coined the new enterprise "BuckEyePuppies.com", but had no photographer in that area. So we loaded the family in the van and just drove around Ohio for a week, checking out Holmes and Wayne counties. One day we prayed "God, help us find a photographer."

That same day, a few hours later, we asked the clerk at a small farm market store near Winesburg, if they knew of anyone who might want to take pictures. They said they did not, but would take our info. That was the only place we asked, at that point, on our entire trip. That evening I got a call from Rob, the fellow that owned the store. He said his daughter "Trista" would be interested taking pictures. She was 15 at the time.

So Trista started working for us. Eventually the store closed. (which was unfortunate) Today, our Ohio office is located in this same building, and Rob, Trista's dad works for us. Trista's husband, Leon, also works for us and manages our Ohio location. Rob also has his own business delivering puppies, which interfaces nicely with BuckEyePuppies.com.

So was this a coincidence? I don't think it was.

Our vehicle for Ohio, which earned the nickname "Pink Floyd." It cost $250 and roared like a banshee, as the exhaust was missing. In hindsight, I do pity Trista for having to drive it! (Ohio has no vehicle inspections)

Looking at land for sale in Alaska—Chapter 4

The seeds of discontentment had been sown, and the winds of change were starting to blow. At first they were only a draft, but after several months they were blowing briskly. Eight or nine weeks later my brother in law, Paul, and his family were visiting at our house in Snyder County. Not much exciting had happened in the meantime, besides the excitement of driving the limo through the local Middleburg parade, and of course our incident with the neighbors.

Paul made the comment "lets look at land prices in Alaska, what could that hurt?" Or maybe I suggested that. Anyway, before we knew what happened, we were browsing real estate for sale in Alaska. It could have stopped at that, but that would have been a tragedy. I found some interesting parcels, and discovered some of them were available under $10,000. It occurred to me that was actually affordable. I casually clicked on the button to email the realtor and requested more information. The seeds had been planted.

Despite requesting information from several realtors, only one, named Carrie, responded with information in a timely fashion. This was not the first time I had explored the idea of buying cheap land in a far flung place, but never Alaska. However earlier searches in other states had led me to land that couldn't be built on, or had various other restrictions. I asked Carrie if I could build a cabin on any of this cheap land. I forget her exact response, but it was to the effect an astonished "why couldn't you build something on it?"

I was then given an education on freedom in Alaska. Having been plagued to near bankruptcy in the past by unreasonable septic system laws, a direct result of the gestapo permit system, I was most interested. When asked if she thought I could shoot a gun on these Alaska land parcels, her response was "this is Alaska." This turned out to be an answer to many questions. Too much freedom at once is a bit overwhelming. But I needed to learn more!!

To be clear: You do not need a permit for a house in Alaska. You do not need a permit for a septic system in Alaska. As long as you are not in town, you can build what you want and do as you please. Think about this for a minute. An entire house-you can just decide to get up one day and build it. No horsing around with permits, inspections, or pleading and groveling with zoning officers for permission to build something on your "own" land.

So began a few weeks of emailing back and forth. I was put on the email list, and was notified every time a new lot was put up for sale. My main requirement was lots of acres, secluded, and cheap. I didn't care if it was near Fairbanks, Homer or Willow. Ironically I ended up buying land in what I consider the best part of Alaska, mostly by accident.

One day a 40 acre parcel for $15,000 caught my eye. The listing showed it had been for sale for years, but I only noticed it then. The wetlands map showed less than half of it to be wetlands, leaving many good acres. This lot was close to the end of a dead end dirt road. It certainly looked promising. Even better, electric service was not run to it, meaning we would need to be "off the grid". Unfortunately there were no good photos of the property.

The realtor lived several hours away. If I wanted to see the property, we would need to fly up there. Flying the whole family up to check it out would have cost over $3,000 – 20% of the sale price of the property. We decided to submit an offer of $10,000 for the property. Unfortunately, our offer was flatly rejected. After our offer was turned down, we thought over this for a day or two. The idea of not getting this property was a hideous one. I decided, why not? People spend $15,000 every day for more stupid things, such as timeshares and PT Cruisers. So we submitted an offer for the full asking price and held our breath.

Soon we got a call from the realtor. The realtor selling the property (not Carrie) was trying to talk us out of it. He explained this property was worse than worthless. Mostly swamp land, and we would need to put in an expensive lane (that observation turned out to be correct) to access the property. I decided if they were trying this hard to talk me out of it, it must be a good deal. I told him I want it anyway. I also decided if I ever sold property in Alaska, I would never use that listing agent.

Who ever heard of trying to talk someone out of buying something they wanted, and you were selling (provided of course it was an honest deal)? The odd thing is I don't think either realtor involved had ever even set foot on the property. In fact, I don't think the owner did either. Much Alaska land is owned by outside investors, and is bought and sold over the phone and Internet. The reason I don't think anyone involved had visited the property is simple: You can see the mountains from it, including Mt. Redoubt and Mt. Iliamna. The mountain rim surrounding Homer is also visible. It also does not have near as much swamp land as they claimed in the listing. $375 an acre was more than a good deal.

In early December 2013 we finally convinced the listing realtor and seller to accept our full price, cash offer with no contingencies. This led to some unexpected medical problems on my part, the main one being insomnia. I would literally lay in bed at night, wide awake. I was so excited I couldn't sleep. We were going to own a piece of Alaska! 40 acres at that!

Marlene and I drove up and down the Sterling Highway many times that month-virtually, on Google Maps street view of course. You get a tour too-check out the last chapter of this book. By the time we actually got to Anchor Point, it looked familiar to us.

This is the only picture we had of the land, a blurry satellite photo (we noticed it had trees on it, so it couldn't be that bad):

Announcing our Purchase to Relatives

Chapter 5

Such exciting news as purchasing Alaskan wilderness can't be kept a secret. I was a bit worried about my parents response though. They don't always think through such an exciting proposition, and as a result, may come to a premature conclusion that it is a bad idea. So one Saturday when they were visiting, I casually mentioned I had 40 acres of pure Alaskan wilderness under contract, and would be closing on it shortly. Instead of wild cheers and hugs, there was stunned silence, like we had just announced we had joined a cult.

I think my Dad said something like "ah, you won't move there, will you?" Despite having been an over the road truck driver for several years, he seemed to think 4,000 miles was quite a hike. Efforts to minimize the distance were unfruitful. So I promised to buy them airline tickets. This seems to make the situation worse (neither my mom or dad had ever flown before). I attempted to appeal to my Dad's "prepper" tendencies, pointing out that Alaska would be the perfect place to hide in the event of Armageddon. I think he said something about "freezing to death", and the conversation went downhill from there. My mom started suggesting that I inherited portions of mental illness from certain ancestors. Oh boy, like I can do anything about that. I guess you can't make everyone happy.

My parents shouldn't have been completely surprised by this Alaska development. Several years ago I gave a Winchester .300 Magnum rifle to my dad for Christmas (following the correct legal procedures). A .300 Mag isn't the largest rifle in the world, but it is larger than anything needed for shooting game in Pennsylvania. When he received the gun, I told him "sometime I'm taking you brown bear hunting in Alaska with that gun." Come to think of it, my mom did act really nervous that day, mentioning fiscal responsibility and such. I think she even gave me a book written by Larry Burkett. This book proved inspirational in purchasing the limo and painting it camouflage, which may not have been what my dear mother had in mind.

Settlement took place January 2nd, 2014. It was done via email, and mailing documents back and forth. Now that I was on the track to be an Alaskan, it was time to think like one. I traded in several guns at the Beavertown Guns & Grocery, and placed an order for a Winchester Model 90 Alaskan .375 H&H Magnum. With Marlene's permission I traded in her pink .22 semi automatic pistol for a more sturdy Taurus .454 Casull revolver.

She claimed she never wanted the gun anyway (it was a Christmas present, I assumed women would like anything pink). I also purchased a .454 Taurus Raging Bull revolver for myself. Yes, we were heading to Alaska. Friends and family started to realize that I was perhaps, serious.

A small concern was the fact our land was just bare land. It had no buildings on it. This didn't bother me any, as I helped my brother in law build pole buildings for two weeks. I was sure we could cobble a house of some sort together. With no permits or inspections to worry about, why anyone can build a house!

It was time to get to know some Alaskans. We attended a Mennonite Church, so naturally I decided it was time to get to know some fellow Mennonites in Alaska. After calling some random people that I didn't know, I got a pattern of names. The first person I talked to was Marlin Eicher. Marlin owns Sterling Supply, in Sterling, AK. In our 2013 visit we had actually stopped in at his place, but he wasn't there. I had talked briefly to his son Dale. Marlin later told me that Dale told him "some weird guy in a limo stopped in". That's ok, Dale.

Since Marlin builds sheds, he was a treasure trove of Alaskan building advice. He also sold metal roofing and some other supplies. During one of our first conversations, Marlin tried to sell me his van. I think he wanted $2,500 for it. It was a fine van, no doubt, but much nicer than what we needed (this is the same van we borrowed later in the book). He mentioned that his wife, Karen, preferred driving the old van over the new van, and you "had to like a woman like that".

Not long afterward I found a Suburban for sale on craigslist for $400. I emailed Marlin and told him "now this is my kind of vehicle." Keep in mind I had never met Marlin in person. Remarkably Marlin agreed to go pick it up for me, pay for it with his cash, and have it waiting there in Alaska for me when I got there. Of course I mailed him a check to cover the cost of the Suburban. I decided pretty quickly that Marlin was a fine fellow! He even managed to get the Suburban price down to $300. When I expressed concern that his wife might want him to keep the Suburban, he assured me that wouldn't be a problem.

On the next page are the actual photos from the original Suburban ad. It's a quality gem all right….

The next fellow I talked to was Alan Reinford. He sells, of all things, ice to Alaskans. He also does excavating, and his wife Twila runs a bake shop. Getting to know Alan and his family proved to be a huge upside to us, although they may have gotten the impression we were parasites until the summer was over (He politely claims they didn't). Over the course of 2014, the Reinford family provided us with lodging, food, roadside service, building site preparation, much advice on Alaska, and even loaned us vehicles, ladders and power tools. He also permitted me to fill up my 275 gallon water tank from his well. Yes, without the Reinford and Eicher families, I believe our attempt to tame the Alaskan wilderness would have been cut short with teary eyes and short tempers.

I explained our plans to Alan, we wanted to build a cabin in Alaska and hopefully live in it. Like most Alaskans, he seemed to think this was a fine idea. His family had lived in a small shed (with no running water) for several months while they built their house. Since this was January, and the ice sales and excavating were slow, Alan agreed to run down to Anchor Point and scope out our land. I told him I wanted a building pad put in, and supplies hauled in as well. Alan lives in Soldotna, which is about a 45 minute drive north from Anchor Point on the Sterling Highway. The drive however feels more like 10 minutes, as there is endless mountain views, ocean, and moose to look at. The one evening when we drove from Soldotna to Anchor Point we counted over 20 moose grazing alongside the road.

At this point I started to plan our cabin design. I wanted something simple and cheap. The idea was to build a cabin, live in it for awhile until we could scratch enough money together to build a house. Then we would rent the cabin out to tourist and visitors. I also planned on building several more cabins to rent out, perhaps by the time this book is published and you are reading it we will have several for rent. As of writing this we still only have the cabin. But who knows, maybe we will start a farm instead. I do have a soft spot in my heart for selling chickens.

I was excited at the prospect of seeing our land, if only in photos. At this point I had not seen anything of it besides satellite pictures on Google Maps. Sure enough, the one day Alan sent me about a dozen pictures. To me, this seemed as exciting as the first pictures of Mars sent back by the mars rover. Alan also picked out what seemed like a good spot for the cabin. I told him to pick the 2nd best spot, as the first spot was to be reserved for our house. Turns out, he did exactly that. On a clear day Mt. Redoubt looms large right out the front windows. Mt. Redoubt is an active volcano, but has not erupted since 2009.

On a side note, when my mom heard we had purchased land in Alaska, all she could talk about was the "Ring of Fire" (and bears). I assumed this was some kind of wild exaggeration, birthed from the paranoia that goes with being a mother. But mom was right about this one. The "Ring of Fire" is a circle around the globe which is prone to earthquakes and volcanoes. When I asked Alan about earthquakes, he laughed and said "oh yeah, we get them all the time." 90% of the worlds earthquakes and 75% of volcanoes are in the Ring of Fire. Our 40 acres sits directly in the so called "Ring of Fire." But so does the whole Kenai Peninsula. I guess if life was predicable, it would be boring?

As I designed the cabin and planned it's construction, Marlene kept bringing up annoying details. For example, "where would we sleep while building the cabin?" "Where would we take showers?" "How would we get to the cabin after the swamp melted?" Etc, etc. I told her not to worry, these details would work themselves out. She didn't seem very comforted by my assertions.

Spenards Building Supply was located just down the road from Alan, so I ordered my lumber from them. Our official right away to access our 40 acres ran through a swamp, which is what the realtor was harping about. Before the snow all melted and the ground thawed, Alan and some of his friends hauled all our cabin lumber in via snowmobile. This took several trips. He also hauled in the tin for the roof, and some custom rough cut lumber I ordered from Calvin Yoder, who runs a sawmill in Sterling.

Unfortunately, I was not yet aware of the time honored Alaskan tradition of burying a vehicle for a septic tank, so I had Alan install a 500 gallon steel septic tank for the cabin. He put in a drain field out of crushed stone, and put down out a stone pad to build the cabin on. This all had to be done before the spring thaw. I also discussed our lane problem with Alan. He made some quick notes, and figured out that running a lane 2,000 feet through the muskeg (a fancy Alaskan term for "swamp") would be outright ghastly. And another complication was that muskeg is wetlands, and in order to do anything with wetlands, you need a permit. I was devastated-here I had planned to flee 4,000 miles to avoid having permits, and now I needed one for just a driveway (but nothing else).

Another barrier to putting a lane in the swamp was the Army Cor of Engineers. They were the ones that issue the permits, and needed to do a wetland study, and all kinds of (expensive) things. For the time being we decided we would just walk over the muskeg to access our cabin. This idea proved to be about as stupid as planning to hire flying horses. It did occur to me that walking through the swamp might not be efficient, so I mailed the owners on the lot beside and in front of mine a letter. This letter requested permission to temporarily access my land through their property.

Around March, I convinced my brother Josh to make plans to fly up and help build the cabin. This wasn't hard to do. All I had to do is ask him if he wanted to spend a month in Alaska with free food and board. Shortly after asking him, on 3/16/2014, I received this email:

"Just bought my (round trip) ticket to Alaska for $377. Really cheap, but the flight is only getting into Anchorage at 6:57 pm on April 30. I could just sleep there that night and you could pick me up the next day if you don't want to drive back to Anchor Point overnight. I'm returning on Monday, May 26. I gotta be at the airport in Anchorage at 8:11 pm. Hopefully this all sounds good because I already bought the ticket. And it's screaming cheaper than leaving and getting back on Saturdays or Sundays. I'm getting pumped already!"

I was glad to hear that, as building a cabin by myself sounded pretty stressful. Josh is not a builder, but he is good at wiring things together. Between the two of us we could make something work. When my mom expressed concern that I would blow the cabin up with leaking propane lines, I assured her Josh would be there to help. She replied "He doesn't know anything either!" The date for our departure was set for April 24, 2014. We would attempt to time our trip to arrive in Anchorage at the same time Josh did, and pick him up at the airport.

On our return trip we would drive the limo. The limo is big, but not big enough for all the items we wanted to move to Alaska. I did make an agreement with a fellow to rent our Middleburg, Pa, house, and part of this agreement was to let all our furniture in the house. Don't tell the renters, but our furniture mostly came from second hand outlets and was not worth the hassle of hauling. But we had a lot of other items too besides furniture, such as power equipment and building supplies.

These were my original plans for the cabin. I actually purchased some design software to design the cabin. In retrospect the design is simple enough to just draw on a napkin, but I was excited and wanted to make sure I "did it right." You can see some differences in the first design and the actual cabin. The laundry room ended up being stuck on the side of the cabin, and all the bathroom fixtures were combined with the laundry room. The roof tin was used, and not shingles. The window layout was changed to accommodate the cheap set of windows I got off of craigslist.

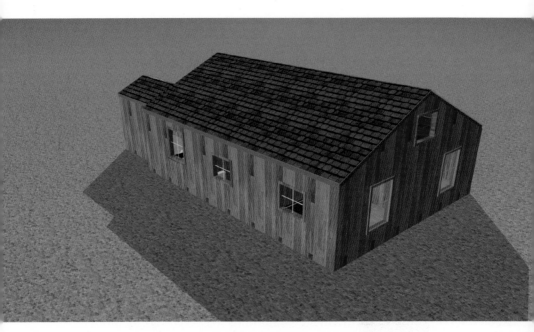

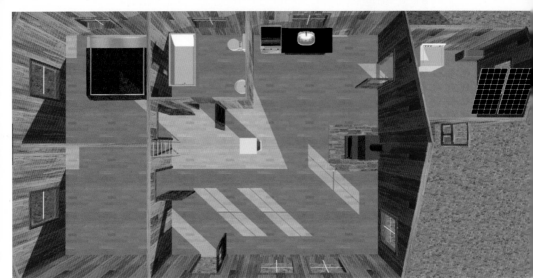

Why I prefer Alaska...

Pennsylvania Resident

Rural Alaska Resident (nothing listed above applies)

First pictures of our property, taken by Alan Reinford

Return to Alaska

Chapter 6

April 24 dawned cool and rainy. I had been up late loading and packing. At this point I was mentally kicking myself for agreeing to take Josh's dual sport motor cycle along. In addition to Josh's cycle, I had a large cast iron wood stove, 400 pounds of flooring (I calculated the weight later), a generator, spare tires for the limo, gas cans, nails, power tools, solar panels, deep cycle batteries, and an assortment of other things. Marlene pointed out before we left that I was asking an awful lot out of the little trailer. "Nonsense" I replied. "This thing is rated for 1,700 pounds."

Finally, we had everything loaded, packed, strapped, and tarped down. The limo was sagging terribly. After I started it up, the suspension filled the air bags with air and it didn't look so bad. We decided to eat lunch on the road, so we called in an order to "Amy's Frosty Freeze", which was only a few miles from our Pa house, and right along the way.

The limo bumped and lurched out our lane. It pulled harder than it ever had before. I would have been nervous, but the mechanic had told me the limo had a truck transmission and rear axle. I carefully pulled out onto Route 104 and headed through Penn's Creek. About a mile after Penn's Creek I looked in the rear view mirror. Something looked funny back there, but I couldn't put a finger on it. Was the tire smoking? Then there was a "POP", and rubber flew everywhere! Oh horrors, and I had just put this brand new tire on yesterday. I pulled off a side road, near Martin's Small Engine Repair.

Getting out and assessing the situation, the tire and rim were both ruined. As I stood there looking at it, deciding what to do next, the remains of the tire burst into flames! I shouted for Marlene to bring me some bottled water, and I hastily doused the tire with water. It took several attempts before the fire was out. In the middle of all this carrying on, someone from the Tool Repair shop across the street came running over, to see if we needed help. He helped me jack up the trailer and put the spare on. Then Marlene reminded me of the food we had ordered at Amy's. Marlene called them and told them of our sad plight, while I wrenched away at the trailer. The people at Amy's were most helpful and brought the food right out to us.

It appeared we had loaded the trailer to heavy, and the fender was scraping the tire, which caused it to explode. Not having many options right then, we just took the fender off the trailer. At this point I decided this trailer was perhaps overloaded and we needed to ditch a few things. So we drove around the block, heading back to our house. Only a few hundred yards down the road, the tire on the other side of the trailer blew out! This was not what I had planned on. I had just burned through $120 worth of tires and rims, and we had only traveled about 4 miles. The rim was already ruined on the tire that just blew out, and I was tired of sitting beside the road. We slowly drove back to the house, with our one good tire and one flat tire, seriously annoying the other drivers behind us.

Back at the house, I started unloading the trailer, and sent Marlene off to look for more tires. She found some at Tractor Supply. I decided the cast iron wood stove and Josh's cycle would have to stay in Pa. This wasn't all bad, as later my cousin traded me an SKS rifle and a snapping turtle for the stove. The snapping turtle part wasn't planned, it escaped out of the back of his pickup while at my place and ran off. SKS rifles are legal to hunt with in Alaska, actually the only thing you can't use for hunting up there is machine guns. It was bad for Josh though, as later someone stole his cycle. But that was after he took it back to his place (in Reading, PA), a few weeks later, so it wasn't my fault. Josh wanted to drive it back to Pa from Alaska. After an hour and a half Marlene returned with tires, and I had the trailer repacked and loaded.

And finally, we were off. By then I was pretty tired out, literally, and the excitement of the trip wasn't nearly as sparkly and fresh as it had been earlier. But I was still excited and glad to be on the way! The rest of the drive in the U.S. was smooth sailing, with the exception of failing to take Kallia seriously when she said she had to go to the bathroom.

We crossed into Canada at a dumpy little town called "Portal" or "North Portal." We crossed over in North Dakota. This was the toughest border crossing yet. We had to go into their building, and were asked a bunch of questions. Then I had to pull the limo into a large ware house, and guards searched through the entire Limo and trailer. I was asked quite a few questions about the guns I had (I did not have any guns along-I had shipped them up to Alaska before leaving). When I mentioned, after being asked, I owned a .223 rifle the guard about flipped a lid (AR-15's, which are illegal in Canada, are common in the .223 caliber). I assured the guard I used my rifle for hunting and not shooting people. At this point I thought it best to discuss my bolt action, Canadian friendly .223 and get off the topic of AR-15's (Pennsylvania only allows manually operated rifles for hunting, so I also have a bolt action .223 rifle for hunting).

I felt bad for the guards having to pick through a few days worth of fast food trash, generated by the children. The guards did not find any contraband in the car or trailer. They were actually polite and helpful (after getting off the .223 subject), and did their best to assist packing everything back up. Of course I didn't have any contraband along, but it is still nerve racking when your car gets searched. For example, what if you had syringes from giving your animals vaccines in your car. Or a box of bullets under the seat that you forgot about, and didn't declare. That would get you a lot explaining to do. Also, don't try to cross into Canada if you have had a DUI in the last few years. They treat that as a very serious offense and will probably deny you entry.

All this time the little trailer had quietly tagged along, content with the excitement it had caused at the start of the trip. It must have had a thing against Canada, because not long after crossing the border it blew a tire out. And another. And another. We started shopping at every Canadian tire along the route. By the time we had reached Tok, Alaska, we had blown 7 trailer tires, and ruined a few rims.

We also had an incident near Grand Praire, Alberta. The limo blew a rear tire, and about killed me when I tried to change it. I'll let you read about that in the included blog post.

Chalk up one more lesson on the road of life-forget the little pretzel jacks. I now carry a 3 ton floor jack around in my vehicles when I travel. A 3 ton jack might be overkill, but it was on sale for $89 at Harbor Freight, and they shipped it to my door for $6! How can your resist a deal like that?

The above location is also in the first book-can you find it? Below: The trailer tires, despite being little, would sometimes blow with surprising intensity!

Limo blows a tire, attempts homicide, a guy named Paul comes to the rescue

Submitted by on Mon, 04/28/2014

This year, I thought I was prepared for the Alaska trip. I thought I could be a role model for the "Be prepared" song that the flying goat sings in "Hoodwinked". After all, I had a tire repair kit along, an air compressor, 2 spare tires for the limo, and 2 for the trailer. I also had 3 jacks, and assorted tools, a second battery located in the limo trunk, and a 2,500 watt inverter to run the air compressor and whatever else needed run.

So, when the familiar sight of rubber and smoke flying out the side of the car occurred, I just laughed and pulled over to the side of the road. Well, I didn't actually laugh, because a $200 rear tire had just lost all it's value, thanks to a faulty tire plug that failed. However, I thought I had the situation under control.

Like I did many times before on the prior Alaska run, I took out a jack, put it under the frame rail, and cranked it up. Only this time, as the jack approached full height, the car shifted and fell off the jack, twisting the jack into a worthless shape and causing the car to come crashing back down on the ground. I was a bit shocked by this development, because I was jacking the car up on level ground, on black top, and everything had seemed solid.

It was fortunate that I did not have any body parts located under the car, as is sometimes the case when working with vehicles. Marlene was lamenting the fact that she could have been left alone, in the middle of Alberta. When I reminded her that I wasn't real crazy about being stuck under the limo, crushed to death, she responded "at least you would be in a better place", while she would have the work of getting a tow truck (if your reading this mom, don't worry, people hardly ever get killed by cars falling on them).

The issue was the automatic leveling suspension. When I jacked up the frame, it deflated the rear airbags, attempting to level the car. This caused the car to shift, since all the weight on the back of the car settled on the jack. As I puzzled over why this never happened before when I changed tires. I realized that last year, before our tire troubles began on that trip, I had disconnected the airbag power line, and hooked it to the fuel pump instead (because the power wire to the fuel pump was having issues), essentially shutting down the auto leveling system.

As I stood there, trying to figure out how to jack this car up without getting killed, I told Marlene "I wish I had a floor jack." Marlene was now insisting that any further attempts at jacking up the car be done without reaching or crawling underneath the car. As I was debating how impractical this was with Marlene, a fellow named Paul (not Paul Harvey) showed up. He announced that he lived across the street, and had been watching our sad situation unfold, and offered his floor jack for us to use. We gladly accepted, and soon the Limo was on road again.

A floor jack can lift directly up on the axle, which does not interfere with the operation of the air bags.

If you happen to read this Paul, thanks so much for you help!

Above: Just outside Grande Prairie, Alberta. Below: The now familiar "Welcome to Alaska" sign.

At approximately 6:45 on April 30th, we rolled into Anchorage International Airport. Not bad timing for a 4,400 mile trip. I called Josh on his cell phone, and he confirmed that he had just landed. Fifteen minutes later he came walking out the gate. Unlike my parents, Josh was ecstatic about visiting Alaska. He even went shopping for land before he left.

After a supper at Denny's, we hit the road south. We drove down highway 1 along the inlet, and Josh appeared to be enjoying the scenery. By the time we arrived in Soldotna, we were all struggling to stay awake. It was nearly midnight, and the only thing we could find open was the "Duck Inn." Their prices were cheap, and they didn't seem to care how many children we packed in the room. So, I was ok with that.

The following morning, we finally got a chance to meet the people I had been talking with and emailing. Our first stop was Marlin Eichers, where we picked up my AR-15 rifle I had mailed up (AR-15 rifles are legal for hunting with in Alaska). There I also got to inspect our fine Suburban for the first time. It was a little rustier than the pictures, but that was just character. Marlin also made the comment he was a little fearful for his life when driving it the few miles to his place (he is so dramatic).

Talking to people on the phone, but not knowing what they look like in person does funny things to your mind. For some reason, I expected Marlin to be short. When he walked in, I almost fell over. He was very tall! So much for preconceived ideas. Marlin and his family started offering us all kinds of things to take along down to Anchor Point. A tent, a propane heater, and I'm not sure what else. "Wow" I thought, "I should have thought of these things before!" He even offered us a 4 wheeler and power tools. After deciding to loan his tent, fire ring, and propane heater, I told him we would be fine, already feeling like I had pillaged his garage.

Next, we swung into the Reinfords. Alan wasn't home, but Twila was. My .454 Casull revolvers were there, I had shipped them up via UPS. Assuming our land would be crawling with large, hungry bears I wanted to take no chances. Twila also loaded us up with baked goods. I had a feeling this just might work out. Then Twila casually made a statement, that had a profound effect on our trip. "We have an apartment you can use" she said. "In case you need a place to stay." I did my best to act like I was reluctantly thinking this over. "Hmm, I'll have to check with Marlene" I said. Twila told us we would need water, and loaned us several large water jugs.

And finally, we were minutes from seeing our very own Alaskan land in person. Excitement ran high as we cruised down the last stretch of the Sterling Highway. Approaching Ninilchik, I noticed a small coffee shop called "The Buzz." Later I would discover this small coffee shop had the best coffee in Alaska. Their pumpkin lattes were especially wonderful.

At last, we turned onto Tall Tree Avenue. I had looked at aerial photos many, many times, but that still wasn't the same as being here. A mile or so in, coming the other way we met an Alaskan bushman type looking fellow. He stopped to chat, and seemed intrigued why we were driving a camouflage limo down his dead end dirt road. When I explained I had bought some property in this road, he knew exactly where I was talking about. He explained he was my new neighbor, and his name was Ron. Then he asked if I brought guns along. My heart sank, because I was worried that he was going to tell me not to make noise, or to leave the guns in Pa. But, no, not so.

Ron explained that if I did not have guns along, we would gladly loan me some, because it was crazy to be out here without guns. The problem is not so much bears, he said. "The moose will stomp you to death." Later he commented "Gunfire is the sound of freedom." I decided I had indeed picked a good neighborhood. When he learned I did not have a .22 caliber long rifle along for shooting spruce chickens, he brought over his Rugar 222 and insisted I borrow it. Ron turned out to be a very valuable wealth of local Alaskan knowledge.

After navigating several S turns, we came to a muddy lane that Ron had described. This muddy lane was our only access to our land, besides the swamp. And I didn't have permission to use the muddy lane, which was actually an old logging trail, because the fellow that owned it had never responded to my letter. Ron explained that while he couldn't give us permission to use the lane, because it wasn't his, but whoever owned it probably wouldn't care. "It's not posted" he said. And besides "this is Alaska." After some discussion we reasoned that the owner of this logging trail probably didn't care if we used it, or they would have at least responded to my letter and told us not to. Ron also mentioned that if they did care that we used the lane, something like Banana Crème Pies would quickly make them happy again.

Since the muskeg was considerably more swampy than I anticipated, our only reasonable option at the time was to try out the muddy logging trail. Parking the limo and trailer, we hiked back through the trail. Our cabin building site was about 2,000 feet off the road. The weather was perfect, the sky a clear blue. It was a warm 65 degrees, with a pleasant wind, birds singing, and the children laughing and running. In the distance we could see stunning snow capped mountains. I felt like we had pried open the door to paradise and climbed in.

Soon, I saw a pile of lumber with a tarp over it. Sure enough, here was the stone pad that Alan had put in. And hopefully enough lumber to build a cabin, because it would be like pulling teeth to transport more in. After the thrill of the moment wore off, it was time to get to work unloading the trailer. Before long, I started realizing that a 4 wheeler was not a luxury in this country. Before a day had passed, we swallowed our pride and also borrowed Marlin's Honda 4 wheeler.

Josh, Marlene and I setup a nice camp spot, beside the cabin pad, and pitched Marlin's tent. The fire ring turned out to be a fantastic idea, because the neighbor casually mentioned without one we would be likely to start wild fires. I found out later that he wasn't kidding. When our relatives heard we were planning to sleep in the Alaskan wilderness, in a tent, they acted with severe consternation (I guess they thought we were staying in a motel or something). Our explanations that the moose were the scary animals to avoid, and the fact they didn't just randomly jump on tents didn't help. This situation escalated when they heard I left a pack of bacon laying out over night. Later, when my parents visited, I made the mistake of letting a "Alaska Bear Attacks" book lay on the table. That was kind of like watching "Jaws" when you're out swimming.

We stayed down at Anchor Point that first night, Friday night, May 2nd, 2014 to be exact. Marlin's tent was divided into 3 sections. Marlene and I stayed in the middle, the girls in another, and Josh and Shane in the 3rd section. I kept a loaded .454 beside my head. Josh also kept the second one in his tent. The first night I must admit I was a bundle of nerves. We were laying on an air mattress, and any second I expected to see a bear paw come through the side of the tent and tear a hole in the mattress. The worst was when nature called at 2am. I poked my head outside in the frigid air, and cautiously shone a flash light around, before exiting, gun drawn, barrel first. These many night time excursions all proved uneventful, except one time when a moose snorted at me and walked off. I almost wet my pants on the spot.

Cabin construction begins, concerned neighbor offers to loan guns

Submitted on Fri, 05/02/2014

Today we rolled into Anchor Point, Alaska, and finally seen first hand our property that we purchased several months ago over the Internet. Turns out, it wasn't a scam after all (some folks, ahem, had expressed doubt that I had actually bought real land, but was duped by Nigerian scammers). It has real dirt, real trees, and hopefully real moose sometime. The stone pad was there, as was our lumber and supplies that we ordered. And I even convinced Marlene to give tenting a shot-starting Friday night. Of course that will end once our fine cabin construction is finished. Tonight we are staying at Alan's place, the fellow that did the excavating for me, and hauled the supplies in on his snow mobile a few weeks before.

I have to admit, I could hardly be more thrilled. The property looks different in person, but you can see snow capped mountains all around, which I think is awesome. I met the neighbors, who were very friendly folks. One neighbor asked if I brought firearms along. I was worried perhaps he might be some anti gun type, until he started explaining how you need guns to stay alive in the wilderness, and even offered to loan a rifle or shotgun to me. My kind of guy! Although he thought hunting rabbits with an AR-15 was overkill. He also detailed on the various stages a moose will exhibit before charging and stomping you to death. Good things to know.

I strapped on my .454 Taurus revolver as soon as we arrived. But I have to admit, after lugging that thing around all day, I'm starting to think a smaller gun might not be a bad idea. But hey, it will help burn some flab down if nothing else.

Like to ride horses? One neighbor has several horses and gives horseback tours. His website is www.AlaskaDraftHorse.com. Desiree (my daughter) loves horses, so we might have to give those horses a workout.

Be blessed,

Matt

The biggest issue with sleeping out in Alaska in early May is the cold. Often the ground would be frozen when we woke up. We had a small propane heater to use, but we were careful with that in the tent because we didn't want to gas ourselves to death. Marlene said she was "so cold her bones hurt." I was very impressed with Marlene's fortitude. The children seemed to thrive in the camping environment, and didn't seem to mind the conditions.

Our muddy lane was over ¼ mile long and slogging back forth proved exhausting. The next day we found ourselves at Marlins again, borrowing his 4 wheeler. He explained he wouldn't miss it, "as the girls just use it to get the mail." I didn't ask the girls what they thought. Marlin also loaned us his trailer, which still had Tennessee plates on it. (they had wisely moved up from TN a few years back) This didn't bother me any, I was just glad it had a plate. The 4 wheeler vastly improved our setup. I was so impressed with Marlin's 4 wheeler, I bought 2 before the year was over.

Before heading back down to Anchor Point, we did what became a common ritual, stopping at Spenard's to buy supplies we forgot. Usually something small, like nails, 2x6's, etc. We also shopped at the Home Depot

Above: Our tent site, beside the lumber pile. Below: Just starting to drag all our things in the long muddy lane and unpack. Desiree appears shocked by something...

in Kenai, but that took longer to round up what we needed.

On Sunday, we visited Sterling Mennonite Church, in Sterling. Here, I finally got to meet the many folks I had talked to on the phone. There was Luis, the fellow with the sled dogs. Calvin, Luis's dad, who had the sawmill. The folks at Sterling Mennonite Church were very friendly and accommodating, and treated us like normal people. This despite the fact we would show up in a camouflage limo, which is unusual at any church, but even more so at a conservative Mennonite one.

We started working out a basic schedule for sleeping arrangements. Weekends we would stay at the Reinford's, because they were much closer to church than Anchor Point. We would often sleep 2 nights in the tent during the week, then 1 night at the Reinfords. After a pleasant weekend at the Reinfords, it was time to get to work on the cabin. Monday, May 5th, was our first real day of working on the cabin.

Figuring we were in an earthquake zone anyway, we decided to just build the cabin on what is called "pier blocks." Seasoned builders reading this are probably clutching their heads in pain at the thought. A pier block is basically a fancy concrete block, with an adjustable metal bracket sticking out the top. Your treated 4x6 sits on top of this. This allows you to adjust the height any time, to compensate for soil settling, frost heave, etc. We did have a stone pad of 2+ feet thick stone to set it on, so I hoped the frost heave would be minimal. I am writing this in January, and so far it has proven to stay level.

After laying down the pier blocks and treated lumber, we started framing up the floor joists. This all took longer than I thought it should, but it was important to get it level and square (according to my brother Josh). Marlin was taken aback when he heard we were using hammers instead of air nailers. I assured him we would be fine. Tuesday afternoon, I think it was, I got a call from Marlin. He told me Wednesday him and his son Dale would be down to help. You have to realize in Alaska people don't work much in the winter. Then in the summer everyone works like wild horses. So if someone volunteers to help for a day in the summer, that's worth like 2 or 3 times as much as it would be in the lower 48.

In the meantime I found some windows on craiglist. A whole house worth of windows for only $250! I figured out I would have spend $2,000 or more buying them new at Home Depot. So we picked up these windows and decided we could make them work.

The floor slowly takes shape. You can see the "pier blocks" in the above photo. With wind, 5 children, and construction waste, our construction site looked like a mess!

With 20 hours of daylight each day, construction went pretty fast. Of course, we were mostly hampered by ignorance of basic construction principles.

The "lane" went from bad to horrible. The only way to get through was full throttle! And even then, lots of pushing. We were very thankful for the Honda 4 wheeler and trailer.

One day Marlene drove the Limo and trailer to get lumber, by herself!
The children loved everything-they soaked it up, there were no boring
moments.

Moosetracks: Not just an ice cream flavor

Submitted on Thu, 05/08/2014

Today my friend, Marlin Eicher, (visit his website at AlaskaSterlingSupply.com) showed up with some automatic guns that really sped up the construction process. Air nail guns, that is. He also brought a large air compressor, nails, and a 6,500 watt generator to get the ball rolling. Thanks to his advice as well, we avoided several construction mistakes that were in the process. Not to be outdone, Rissler Garage Doors, located near Ephrata, Pa, dispatched their very own company president and CEO to fly up and help out (the company president also happens to be my brother in law).

Back to moose tracks. We keep discovering moose tracks on our land, but no moose yet. I did see 6 moose this evening on my way to Soldotna from Anchor Point. The moose have ample opportunity to leave tracks on our land in Anchor Point, right now it's very, very muddy. The other morning I got my socks that were drying all night, and was dismayed to discover they had a silty, foul smelling texture. The last 2 days have been pretty rainy, as you can see in the pictures... our lane is nothing but a mud pit right now. The result is the humane society would complain about the living conditions in our tents, if we had any dogs in them (we do have some generous friends that allow us the use of their facilities).

Cabin construction has been going well, we finally have a wall up. Tomorrow we hope to get a few more walls up, and perhaps we may have the roof sheeting on this weekend. However my time estimates have been woefully off, so time will tell.

I have lost track of the amount of times we have gotten the four wheeler stuck. But that's ok, it keeps things from getting boring.

Also, I just heard a true story about a fellow up here in Alaska who was charged by a Grizzly bear. He shot it 11 times with a .300 Winchester Magnum before it finally dropped, close enough for him to kick it. Makes my little 6 shot .454 sound rather inadequate.

There is more land for sale here in Alaska, come on up!

Matt

The Cabin Walls Go Up

Chapter 7

Wednesday morning Marlin and Dale showed up. And wow, they brought the whole shop along. Air nailers, a huge generator, saws, air compressor, hoses, ladders, the whole nine yards (did you know that saying comes from World War II, the P-51 Mustang held 36 feet of laced .50 caliber machine gun ammunition. If they emptied their guns on a target it got the "whole 9 yards"). Marlin wasn't there long before he noticed some mistakes we had already made in the building construction.

As I was returning with the 4 wheeler, I had ran back to the end of the lane for something, I saw Marlin, Dale, and Josh tearing up the plywood floor we had just nailed down. Turns out we were putting the plywood down the wrong way. I'm glad they showed up before we put the walls up! Things happened fast with professional builders on the scene. Marlin also showed us how to properly frame in windows and doors. I really don't know what we would have done without Marlin and Dale's help. It was even rainy and miserable that day, and that didn't stop them.

It was exciting to see the walls go up. We felt like we were actually getting somewhere. When Marlin went to leave, he said to just keep his equipment until we were finished. I must admit that using an air nailer really grew on me. It sure sped things up, and I even bought two for myself after I gave his back. Marlin left enough tools at the cabin to power a work crew. A huge air compressor, generator, several ladders, an air nailer. Of course, his 4 wheeler, gas cans, saw, and many more things. A week or so later he even showed up with his skid loader (I haven't bought one of those yet).

Despite the almost 24 hour sunshine, we had a bad habit of sleeping in, even while sleeping on the ground. It might have something to do with the fact it never got really dark. You would work and work, and think, wow I'm tired. Then you would check the time and discover it was 11pm. I often was up until 2 or 3 in the morning, just because it didn't seem right to go to bed when it was still daylight out.

So, the one morning I woke up, and everyone else was still sleeping like logs. I yelled and made noise, but nobody stirred. Then I noticed my AR-15 sitting on a stack of lumber. Unloaded, but with a full 30 round magazine laying next to it. "Hey, why not, we are in Alaska" I thought. So I popped in the clip, chambered a round, pointed it at the dirt pile, and emptied it as fast as I could pull the trigger.

This got immediate, effective results. People started popping out of tents like ping pong balls. "Was it a bear?!" someone shouted. Nope, just time to wake up.

Thursday I talked to my brother in law Harlan, and found out that he was going to fly up the next Monday and help out. My father in law almost flew up with him, but backed out claiming "he was too old for Alaska" (I'm pretty sure while in Alaska, I saw people older than him up there).

This was a huge plus, as we would soon be ready to put the roof on, and Josh and I both were nervous about such things. I also talked with Luis that day, and he said him and his brother Justin were planning to come help on Saturday. This was great timing, as neither Josh or I knew anything about setting rafters either.

The fire ring Marlin loaned us, great for grilling.

Undoubtedly, "real" builders would be horrified by many of our construction techniques, and also have a good laugh about how long it took us to frame things up. However at this point we couldn't help but feel a little pleased with ourselves. This is our progress at about one week. We had mostly great weather, and warm days to work in. A funny thing about Alaska, 55 degrees Fahrenheit is comfortable when the sun is out. I'm not sure why or how, but it is.

"The Buzz" Coffee Shed: The Pope in the Religion of Coffee
By Josh Snader

Coffee is everywhere. If you showed up uninvited to a research center in Antarctica, I'm guessing you could get your hands on a hot cup of coffee in several minutes. The coffee might be terrible but it would fall under the definition of "coffee" thus making my point valid.

Many people, whom I dub "Coffee Snobs," look at me sideways with pompous smirks when I mention that Maxwell House is my standard go-to source of coffee grounds. When you find these coffee snobs in large groups, they inevitably try to outdo each other with the exclusivity of their finely tuned coffee palate. Typically the conversation starts when I walk up holding a white Styrofoam cup full of coffee which I found in a large thermos somewhere.

"Ahhh, Coffee! I can finally wake up now." I fire off the first shot in what will quickly become a large scale ground war of quick retorts and one-upping.

The shot echoes off of the mountain range of heads. Someone wrinkles their nose. "You call this coffee?"

"HAHA!" Someone else deems their opinion more worthy. "This is swill. I grind my own coffee with my gold plated coffee grinder I bought from an impoverished native on the foothills of the Himalayas."

I hear chests being puffed up. The attention shifts to the other side of the group. "OH OH? Every single time I make a cup of coffee I fly to Peru, grow my own coffee beans watered only with holy water from the local monastery, pick them at precisely four o'clock on a sunny afternoon – not when it's cloudy!- and then fly home. I didn't even start to grind them yet! Then.."

I never hear the rest because I usually give up, walk off, and get another cup of coffee before I get caught in a social quagmire of coffee chest thumping.

Continued on next page….

All that just to set this up: I found the best coffee anywhere. Seriously. You can trust me because my coffee standards are so bad. I was once told to drink some Starbucks coffee and "I'll be sold." I did and found out what they meant is that I'll be sold into slavery just so I can afford a cup. It was good but I couldn't tell the difference from the standard cup of McDonald's Joe, honestly. It was just a little stronger. That causes some peoples head to explode. "YOU CAN'T TELL THE DIFFER – POP!" It gets messy so I usually keep my opinions to myself.

However, today I've decided to nail this down once and for all. I found a coffee shop – shed, rather- that is so spectacular that it burst through the layers of crusty residue left on my tongue from years of inferior coffee and lit up my taste buds like napalm on the hills of Vietnam. This coffee is so good that I actually noticed it was good.

The Buzz. It's a coffee shop along Route 1 on the Kenai Peninsula in Ninilchik, Alaska. It's the pope in the religion of coffee. It's so good that this coffee cynic bowed down and – no, OK, it's just coffee. Really good coffee. The best coffee I've ever had. I went back again and again, even starting up a chicken sales website to support my habit. Alaska may be far away but it's easier than flying to Peru to grow your own coffee beans with locally sourced holy water. From now on when I run into Coffee Snobs I'll just be like, "Well, did you have coffee from The Buzz?"

They'll skeptically shake their heads no. "What's the Buzz?"

I'll just look at them sideways with a pompous smirk. "Obviously you've never had good coffee." Yup, it's that good.

Earthquake!
Chapter 8

Saturday morning, May 10, shortly after 6 am I woke up to a banging and clanging. We had slept at the Reinfords that night, and we were in their apartment over the garage. It felt like someone was shaking the house. I heard things falling off the walls down below in the garage. Normally it takes me a few minutes to wake up, but not that morning. Not used to earthquakes, I instantly jumped out of bed, wide awake. Should we run out of the house? Was it about ready to collapse on our heads? Was death imminent?

The earth quake only lasted about 30 seconds, and it had stopped shaking before I really had time to exit the building. I called Alan to ask if I should be worried about the garage falling down. "Don't worry" he said, "that was a little one, the trees weren't bending over." He then proceeded to explain that if you looked out the window, and the trees weren't bending back and forth and almost hitting the ground, it was nothing to worry about. Good to know. I hope I'm never in a tree stand when a big earthquake hits.

Later that morning, around 8:30, Luis and his brother Justin stopped in at the Reinford's. Alan graciously let me borrow his Chevy pickup truck, and we headed down through towards Anchor Point. The inside door latch didn't work, so to open it you needed to roll down the window and unlatch it from the outside. In Ninilchik we stopped at "The Buzz" coffee shop. This was the first time I had actually stopped in there. The coffee was excellent, and it is still my favorite coffee shop (and Josh's too). Although I can't help but think the one guy that works there drinks too much caffeine. Maybe he samples the product often, he talks really fast. He is a very friendly sort.

The topic of discussion at the coffee shop that morning was the earthquake. The epicenter was in Cook Inlet, and the closest town to it was Anchor Point, our town. We were told it was a 5.2 magnitude. I was slightly worried we would get to the cabin and find the walls all knocked down. It did seem the cracks in the road blacktop were wider than the day before, but I'm not sure about that.

When we arrived, the cabin look just like it had the day before. The floor and walls were even still level. Justin brought along his .44 magnum lever action rifle, in case any black bears showed up. He had a black bear tag, and the neighbors claimed there were bears in the area. Unfortunately we didn't see any that day, but we did get a lot of work done.

We got the two bedrooms framed up, and we set the ridgepole running across the middle of the cabin. Luis also setup a rafter pattern to use. We did have a small work place injury, while Luis was attempting to carve out a notch in one of the beams, his chisel slipped and went flying across the cabin. He cut himself in the process as well. Nothing a little antiseptic and band aids didn't fix though.

I didn't know Luis real well yet, and I thought at first he was just kidding around. "Someone could get hurt, flinging that sharp chisel around" I thought. But all was quickly forgiven. Even had it been intentional, it's hard to pass judgement on volunteer help.

Luis worked with a professional dog sled musher over a year, in fact his family claims 4 Iditarod championships (the people he worked for). Luis has his own sled dog team, and I learned a lot about dog sled, huskies and more from him. All the champion Iditarod dogs are actually mixes, of husky, bird dogs, and anything else that runs fast. To date, no team has ever won with "purebred" dogs. Which, if you think about it, "purebred" has only been around for a little over 100 years. There is nothing really purebred about a purebred dog anyway, despite what the kennel clubs say. When the "rubber meets the road" aka in the Iditarod, registration papers are worthless.

Luis tests out his rafter pattern

Monday my brother in law, Harlan, showed up. I expected him to arrive sometime around lunchtime. Instead, I got a call at 8:00 am, he was wondering where I was. His flight arrived in Anchorage around 1am, and instead of getting a motel he just rented a car, drove town to Anchor Point, and slept in it. As I mentioned earlier, Harlan couldn't have showed up at a better time. Josh and I were about as agile on the roof as sacks of moldy potatoes.

Harlan was quite pleased we were ready to set rafters. For some odd reason, he acted like he expected to see stacks of disheveled lumber, and not much else. Hopefully this low expectation had nothing to do with the 2 week stint I did helping him construct pole buildings. Harlan was even more impressed with the rafter design and pattern Luis has but together. I briefly thought about trying to take the credit, but I don't think he would have believed me anyway (and of course that wouldn't have been very nice to Luis).

Harlan could run around the roof in ways I didn't think possible...

Harlan works at nailing the rafters down, while I hand them up. It was hard to keep Shane off the roof. Despite his antics, he did not get hurt even once. The cross beam that Harlan is standing on is rough cut by Calvin Yoder's sawmill. I like the look of exposed rough cut beams.

The rafters are all set, and working on the gable ends.

Below: It was very common to see moose, we saw them almost every day.

I did have a disagreement with Harlan that involved the windows at the end of the cabin. I have found if you get several builders helping on a project, you'll get several opinions, and they are often different. Our big windows on the end of the cabin we had intentionally kept low and under the wall header. Marlin explained it would compromise the integrity of the wall if we had windows going through the header. I agreed, and so we framed it up that way.

Harlan, however, insisted we tear the wall apart and raise the windows 2 feet. He explained how they could be framed up without making the wall unsound. This would take quite a bit of time, and I didn't want to waste quality help moving windows around when we had a roof to put on. Now, when I look at the cabin I wish I would have considered Harlan's advice, but at least the roof is on.

We were finishing up the roof, and I discovered we were one tin piece short. I apparently forgot to measure something somewhere, so we ended up using a blue cover piece in the back. The cover piece is a piece of tin used to protect the rest of the tin in shipping.

I discovered the hard way that you should measure twice, and cut once!!

At this point the interior still needed a lot of work. It was a relief to sleep inside a building for a change. I no longer lay with a loaded gun beside my head and woke up at every slight noise. It was also easier to stay warm at night. The plumbing and electric still need to be installed. Harlan fashioned a makeshift table and some shelves for a primitive kitchen, which was nicer than using stacks of lumber for a table.

Towards the end of the week our family took Harlan and Josh to a fancy restaurant in Homer for some fresh halibut. When impressing people with how delicious halibut is, it is important to select a good restaurant. Poorly done halibut will probably still be the best fish they have ever eaten. Properly done halibut, however, creates an experience that transcends time and space. It is the pinnacle of an earthly culinary experience. If someone eats poorly done halibut, and they hear you rave about it, they will say (or think), "oh it was good, but not as good as you are describing." For the sake of your integrity, if nothing else, take people to a good halibut restaurant. I have never eaten anything better than fresh halibut. Ever.

I normally don't eat at fancy restaurants, so I was a bit startled when the waiter would snatch every bit of trash away as we would create it. You use a napkin, lay it down, and "poof", it's gone! The children were sitting at the table beside us. They must have wore out the waiter, because towards the end of the meal the trash was starting to pile up at their table. At one point in the evening, Harlan was discussing the merits of Alaska's favorite siding, Tyvek. He really got into this, and was discussing various prints that should be available, and fashionable styles for applying it. After about 15 minutes of this animated discourse, the waiter politely asked, in a somewhat incredulous tone, if he was talking about house wrap.

Harlan also helped me mount the solar panels on the cabin, and hookup the batteries and inverter. Our setup initially was really small. It consisted of 2-230 amp hour 6 volt batteries, connected together to make 12 volts. I had a 5,000 watt inverter, that I think came from Harbor Freight (this inverter worked much better than the trailer). The panels were 230 watts each. This setup won't set records, but it was great for charging phones, running the laptop, and other small odds and ends. The batteries, when fully charged, would even run the coffee pot for awhile. I thought that was impressive, as the coffee pot pulls 1,500 watts when brewing. Once we had a refrigerator and water pump running though, the batteries and panels were far from adequate.

Later in the year, we significantly upgraded the system, adding 6 more batteries and 4 more solar panels. Sometime I plan to switch it around to a 48 volt setup instead of a 12 volt. Eventually we'll add more panels as well. There is something really satisfying about running on free electric. I'm not all jacked up on lowering pollution, but I do like the idea of saving money. And if it keeps the air cleaner, that's a nice bonus for sure.

The panels I purchased from Elmer Reihl, of Advanced Energy Products, in Loysville, Pa. I thought about just buying a setup off the Internet, but I didn't know anything about these products. Elmer, being Amish, runs his entire house off of solar panels and batteries. I figured if anyone knows how to make this practical, he would. He programmed the charge controller for me, and set it up so when we got to Alaska we just need to plug everything in. Several folks (from Pa) asked me why I didn't just run electric to the cabin from the power lines. Newsflash: There are no power lines within miles of the cabin.

We also had a 2,000 watt Honda inverter generator that we brought along. This generator performed flawlessly, and sipped gasoline. Part of our setup included a hookup for the generator to charge the batteries. This little generator made remote living much easier. It was also quiet enough to carry on a conversation while standing beside it. After arriving in Alaska, two of the neighbors said "I needed to get a little Honda generator." They all used them and raved about them, which helped me feel good about the purchase. A little Honda like ours runs about $1,000 each.

With the cabin taking shape, we needed furniture for it. Not wanting to take out a loan for something just to sit on, we shopped for some used furniture. There was a fellow in Anchor Point moving to the lower 48, and was selling a lot of items. We ended up buying 2 leather sofas, a kitchen table, and a number of other items from him.

To pickup the sofas we ran the Suburban down to his place, pulling Marlin's trusty trailer. We located the place without any trouble. Then I made a critical mistake, I shut down the engine. It's best to always let your engine run when driving older vehicles around, although this strategy has it's perils as well.

One time I had a 1978 Ford pickup that I left run, while trying to pull another car I had onto a trailer (that car didn't work at all-it had broke down at a friends place). This was the 1990 Ford Crown Victoria that I bought for $300, and managed to drive it an entire year before it ran into more costly issues. We drove it to Florida and Michigan without incident, except one time it ran out of oil. I managed to notice before the engine seized up, as the oil pressure went to 0 and made funny noises (it used a lot of oil—6 quarts to go to Florida).

As I worked to line up the car onto the car dolly, I heard the truck "clunk" into gear, by itself. It also had a habit of revving like a racehorse in idle. This was a bad combination of events. Without hesitation, the truck lurched backward across the parking lot and headed down a bank full of trees. It cleared the bank, and slammed right into the trees, with metal crunching and glass flying. Now I was stuck with two vehicles that didn't work. Arlan, from Clark Hill Service center came out to help pull out the truck, and was almost bit by a snake when he reached under the truck to connect a chain to it (the snake was wrapped around an A arm close to the warm engine).

This all happened behind Weaver's Archery in Middleburg, Pa. I was very glad the truck was pointed towards the woods and not Keith Weaver's archery shop. Anyone that doubts this happened, just ask Keith's children, they saw it all happen. After pulling the truck back out of the trees, I drove it for a few months until Pennsylvania's vehicle inspection doomed it to the scrap yard. All that to explain why I shut the Suburban off. I didn't want it launching into a stranger's house or running over anyone.

Fortunately, I had jumper cables along and we just jumped the Suburban and we were off again with our load of 2 sofas on the trailer. After turning into Tall Tree avenue and going about 2 miles, the Suburban shut off again. It appeared the battery went so dead it caused the vehicle to shut off. I made a mental note to replace the alternator.

It was a nice day, so Marlene and I got out and started walking. The children were all at the cabin with Uncle Josh. The .454 was holstered securely under my jacket, so I was not concerned about bears or wolves. Before we had walked two hundred yards, a fellow pulled up and asked if we needed help. This turned out to be a neighbor named Dale that we had not met before. Dale gave us a jump, and the Suburban purred like a kitten for the last 2 miles of Tall Tree avenue. Like the other neighbors, Dale agreed newer vehicles were a waste of money. It felt good to belong.

I was very pleased with the progress we made on the cabin while Harlan was there. Before he left Saturday night we had all the doors and windows in, the roof on, and a lot of little odds and ends done. It seemed like we were almost done! Then I found out the details are where the problem lies. Things looked like they were moving swiftly, until we came to the interior. Details, such as wiring and plumbing, took longer than I expected.

We also had a looming deadline. June 5th my parents were flying into Anchorage Airport. My mom explained in no uncertain terms that she was not going to be wondering around in woods full of large, dangerous animals, doing her business. That cabin would have a flush toilet-or they were renting a motel room in town and we could have the cabin to ourselves. That demonstrates a phenomenon I noticed from people "outside" (those in the lower 48), they seem to think every stroll in the woods brings you face to face with death and dismemberment. Of course, then you got the other extreme to, nutcases who think you can stroll around with daisy chains and whistle at the bears. The truth is, you'll hardly ever get charged by a brown bear. But when you do, it's nice to have a trump card to play.

Harlan was a huge blessing-this is how the cabin looked after he left. Before he came, no windows, no doors, no roof! Marlin came down the one day and help put the tin on too.

Below is a picture of our first attempt at generating solar power. The first system consisted of (2) 6 volt golf cart batteries, with 230 amp hours each. Below them you can see our 5,000 Watt 12 volt invertor from Harbor Freight. This invertor performed flawlessly. To the right of the batteries you can see our first charge controller. In bright sunlight, this setup would generate 20 amps at 12 volt from our 230 watt panels mounted on the outside.

Because the sun's movements across the horizon are more extreme far north, solar panels are not as efficient further south, unless you can adjust them throughout the day. There is a lot more sunlight though, which makes up for this problem in the summer. In the winter, it makes the problem worse.

It did not occur to me until later that having batteries in the cabin might cause a fire hazard. They also give off gasses that are probably not as good for you as some things. Because of these issues, I want to build a "generator shed" to house the generators and batteries. This will keep them out of the weather, and lower the risk of burning the cabin down. Now our system is up to 8 batteries, so it also takes up a lot more room. It will be nice to get it out of the bathroom.

The bare essentials, don't play capture the flag in our woods

Submitted on Sat, 05/17/2014

Last year, while driving up through the Arctic to Prudhoe Bay, I noticed signs warning folks to pack out their waste, if doing business in the woods. Like the city folks picking up doggy doo, except in this case, your doo. Rest assured, I would rather risk a $10,000 fine than hike around with warm feces sloshing around in my back pack. What about the moose? I didn't notice any of them with packs on their backs. Which brings me to this point: step carefully in our woods. You may notice white flags fluttering in the wind among the underbrush. These are not to pick up. Since our toilet is not yet hooked up, well, you can imagine. And rest assured, we don't pack waste out of here, either.

Ok, enough potty talk. The good news is we have made great progress on the cabin. On Friday we mounted our solar panels, batteries and invertor. I promptly tested out the rig by making coffee. It buzzed through that, no sweat. I'm hoping to run a small refrigerator off our setup, along with some LED lights and my laptop. We'll see how it works out, but so far I'm pretty impressed.

The roof, windows and doors are all installed as well. Right now we are working on the wiring for the cabin, and attempting to install a sand point well. For photos of the progress, check out our American Gun dogs facebook page, or click here.

My brother in law, Harlan, has flown back to Pa. He was here for 5 days, and was a huge asset. I gave him my best sales pitch on Alaska, so hopefully they move up here...

have a great weekend,

Matt   Here are the bare essentials:

Wildfire!

Chapter 9

Sunday, May 18 we decided to go for a hike. It was gorgeous, clear day. We drove down Funny River Road, near Soldotna, to look for a hiking trail. There were several areas with nice trails down that way. We parked along the road and took a nice trail back into the forest. There were large "Warning: Brown Bear Area" signs posted, which I get a kick out of. The picture of the bear on the sign looked like he was ready to eat someone. Naturally, I was packing a .454, so I didn't really care if we did run into bears. My brother, Josh, was along, and he was packing the other .454. Our family had a nice walk, and we didn't see any sign of bears. We didn't smoke any cigarettes or start any fires.

Monday morning we left the Reinford's and drove down to our cabin to work on it. In the afternoon we noticed the sky turning dark. "Looks like a storm brewing" I told Josh. I didn't think they got tornadoes and such up here, but the sky was really looking threatening. We kept working, and despite the ominous clouds looming, it didn't rain. We were working on getting the house wired up. That evening, we switched on the electric lights for the first time. That felt good, to stand beside the light switch, flip it, and watch the cabin light up. Living in the wilderness helps you appreciate things you otherwise wouldn't.

With the cabin structure built, and now with lights and some electric, it was starting to feel like home. We still slept at the Reinford's some, but we were trying to wean ourselves off mooching from them. One problem was, it was still rather brisk at night. We used up lots of those little propane bottles, keeping Marlin's heater going at night. It was great to sleep in the cabin for a change, as I was always a little nervous about being dragged out of my sleeping bag and messily devoured in the middle of the night.

Tuesday I talked to Alan, and he mentioned there was a wild fire burning briskly only a few miles from their place. He said the fire was on "Funny River Road." The exact place we went hiking 2 days before! Oh no, I thought, "they will think we did it, driving around there in that crazy limo the evening before the fire starts." Fortunately, driving an odd looking car around is not grounds for arson, and nobody bothered asking us about it.

The sky got almost black at mid day from the smoke of the fire. Our cabin was at least 30 miles from the nearest point of the fire, but we still had ashes blowing past. It looked a little bit like snow.

Desiree and Kallia relax on the cabin chairs. On the table you can see a hard hat Shane found some where. Below Josh stuffs insulation into the rafters.

Prior page: The site of the Funny River fire, one year later. Above: It must really rattle to hit a moose. Yes, I think those are bullet holes in the sign. We have had 2 close calls (with moose, not bullet holes). Below: The creek where we pump water out for the cabin, "Stariski Creek".

Josh shocked me with his handiwork on the loft ladder and railing, I really didn't know he had it in him. He also painted the cabin a hideous red color, which was my fault. I bought a bucket of stain, and gave it to him without actually checking the color. By the time I realized it was ghastly, he had already done most of the cabin front. No problem, we'll wrap it in Tyvek! (and eventually put wooden siding over it)

Tired of nearly freezing to death every night, we decided it was time to install a stove. There is plenty of firewood on our 40 acres, and free coal at the beach. It only made sense to get a stove that would burn both kinds of fuel. I noticed Spenard's had a cool looking pot bellied stove on sale for $499. It looked like something you would see at Cracker Barrel. Busy trying to plumb and wire the cabin, I sent Marlene up to Spenards with a list.

Marlene returned awhile later and remarked "she was surprised how expensive it was". Wanting to know what she meant, I looked at the receipt. $1,400 dollars! I almost passed out. Marlene was unapologetic about spending so much on the stove. She said "When you are cold, and in Alaska, you do drastic things". Hard as it was to believe, it seemed everything we did was more expensive than I had planned. That is not just an Alaska phenomenon, I noticed this in Pennsylvania as well. Sure that there was a mistake, I carefully checked the receipt. With the wall kit, hangers, and exterior stainless steel chimney, it did indeed cost that much. When I finished, there was one section I didn't need that I was able to return and get $89 back.

Installing the stove went good. It was a little tricky getting all the angles put in the stove pipe, as we wanted the stove more in the corner of the cabin. The stove pipe we ran as close to the peak as we could, so we didn't have to use as much of the expensive stainless steel pipe on the outside to get high enough for a good draft. I learned the hard way, at a previous house, that you must have a good draft. Otherwise you wake up in the middle of the night, choking on smoke. I also learned at that time, using inside stove pipe on the outside of the house is a really bad idea. It lasts about a month, and will fall apart on a windy, cold night.

The stove made it a great deal more comfortable in the cabin. We still didn't have everything insulated, so it cooled down fast if the fire went out. But at least we could get it warm quickly if we wanted. The free beach coal also burned fantastic in the little stove. There is something very gratifying about walking around picking up free hunks of coal. It's almost as good as being able to find free gasoline cans full of gas laying about.

In the picture on the opposite page, you can also see our progress with the tongue and groove paneling and insulation.

That day the black clouds got even blacker, and it looked like it was snowing. That is when we realized the clouds were actually smoke from the fire, and the "snow" was ashes. The Funny River Fire kept escalating, until it was the second largest wildfire in the history of the state of Alaska, according to some sources. Soon, our friends were calling, concerned we were about to be incinerated. Our cabin was not in danger, it was at least 30 miles from the fire. However, the Reinford's were put on evacuation watch. The fire roared within 1 mile of their property, with flames reaching over 300 feet in the air. The weather forecast on Josh's phone said "Smokey".

Wednesday night we decided to stay in Soldotna at the Reinford's, as I needed to pickup some supplies in the morning. When we pulled into their driveway that evening, their motor home was packed and waiting for a quick exit. Twila informed us "we were welcome to stay, but might have to evacuate in the middle of the night". It was a rather strange feeling. The sky was blacker than ever, and it actually got dark that night, unusual for summertime Alaska. But, darkness from a looming wildfire doesn't actually help you sleep better.

We woke up that morning, still at the Reinford's, unscathed. The winds had blown the right way and kept the fire from coming closer. After that scare, it rained the one night, which helped calm the fire down. Heavy fire fighting equipment was also brought in. They called these planes "water bombers". When I seen one flying, it actually looked like a World War II era B-17 flying fortress. Later someone told me they were actually old bomber planes, refitted to fight forest fires. Sometimes the bulldozers would drive into the flames, pushing brush, while the water bombers dropped water on them to keep them cool. I don't think I would like that job.

One family from the Mennonite church in Sterling was evacuated. They could see the forest fire from their house windows. However it did not get close enough to harm their house, and a few days later they could return home. Other families started clearing swaths of trees away from their houses, to reduce the risk of the fire getting close to their houses.

Later in the week, we got some more rain, and the winds cooperated. This did not put out the fire, but calmed it down to the point where it could be contained. It eventually consumed 193,597 acres, or about 250 square miles. By the weekend, no one was worried anymore about the fire.

Sunday afternoon Josh claimed his flight back to PA was scheduled, so we dropped him off at the Kenai airport, after church.

Limo gets stuck in bank drive through, causes small traffic jam

Submitted on Fri, 05/30/2014

A few days ago, May 28th, I believe it was, I had one of my fears come to pass. I have this phobia of getting stuck in a drive through with the limo. Normally I never even try to take the car through a drive through, except for the Burger King in Lewisburg, Pa. That drive through has plenty of room. Considering the limo is almost 30 feet long, I tend to think this is a reasonable fear. To put this in perspective, 30 feet is longer than a quad cab pickup truck with a full length bed.

So we are up in Alaska, building a cabin and very much enjoying our time here. Not because of all the great fishing and hunting, because we only went fishing once for a few minutes, and that was a miserable experience. I'm not sure why I like it so much here (besides 100 obvious reasons), as pretty much the only thing I have done in the last month is work on the cabin. To further my Alaskan experience, I decided to open a bank account at a local bank. The only requirement was that it had "Alaska" in the bank name (because "Alaska" sounds really cool").

So while in Soldotna picking up some supplies, I swung into a bank to setup an account. I don't even remember the name of the bank, but it did have "Alaska" in the name. To my horror, I realized I had pulled into the drive through, and that the drive through lane was not intended for vehicles of any size, much less a limo (you would think they would cater to rich guys in limos who pull through and toss sacks of cash out). I was also pulling a trailer. Now if you never had the chance to feel stupid, I'll loan you my limo with a trailer, and you can go clog up a bank drive through, around noon at the busiest time. This branch also happened to be one of their larger branches, with 4 drive through lanes. Of course all 4 lanes went through one lane first, which was the lane the limo was stuck in.

The only option was to back out. As I was trying to back out, other vehicles kept trying to come into the drive through (another pompous rich guy trying to show off his rig, they probably thought*). After several minutes of backing around, I finally made it back onto the road, and pulled around in another parking lot with much more room.

Despite our performance in the drive through, the bank people were friendly and didn't treat us like lunatics. (although the one teller kept staring at us) The fact we had all 5 children along didn't seem to help.

Back to the cabin again. Turns out the fancy new toilet I installed isn't good enough for the family. The children (and Marlene) kept insisting I install a door on the bathroom. I tried to explain you just shout loudly before entering, to make sure no one is inside, or use the bathroom late at night when everyone else is sleeping. However that system proved faulty and very unpopular. So this evening I finally installed a real door on the bathroom.

One more quick note-this evening I went for a short walk, and scared a moose out of the bushes. I thought that was pretty neat....

Have a great week,Matt

* Actually nobody has ever seemed to assume I'm rich when I pull in with the limo, in fact it almost seems to work the other way. Wearing dirty work clothes does little to improve on this, I discovered.

Our "Home Depot" kitchen cabinets. When we stopped in to pick them up we discovered they were having a 20% off sale on just cabinets. That was nice! Shane shows off for the camera...

We were at Alan's later that Sunday afternoon, when Josh called. He had arrived safely in Anchorage, but the problem was his flight was not scheduled until Monday evening. Thankfully, the airline switched some things around, and he was able to fly out Sunday evening anyway. I don't think he likes keeping airline schedules, this wasn't the last time he would wreak havoc on airline schedules.

Josh's ride to Anchorage from Kenai airport

May 28, I got this email from my mom "Dad is in the York Memorial Hospital ER, he got really sick while driving truck, he was on his way back to Raytec from Baltimore. Waiting to hear more. Dr. talked about admitting him. Pray for him." Talk about a deal breaker! They were scheduled to fly into Anchorage June 5th, and the tickets are nonrefundable. I still didn't have the toilet hooked up, but I didn't tell mom that.

I tried calling my dad, and he didn't answer the phone. He was admitted to the hospital, and a day later I tried calling him again. He answered, but acted completely "out of it." He was on some kind of wild pain killer medication. Now I was feeling more worried about him than the plane tickets. After all, you can always buy more tickets. In the meantime, I decided I would put the pressure on getting the plumbing working, just in case. I still clung to some hope they might be able to fly up.

A few days later, we started getting some good news. Dad had an infection in his leg, causing it to swell up. But he was on medication that was dealing with it, and it seemed to be working. They might be able to make it to Alaska after all. The day before they were scheduled to leave, my dad had an appointment with his doctor. He had been released from the hospital a few days earlier. As the doctor was checking out his leg and making small talk, my Dad asked if he could fly to Alaska tomorrow. "What?" the doctor asked. He repeated his question. "I guess, just make sure your close to a hospital up there" was the doctors reluctant reply. Talk about encouraging advice. The hospital in Homer is about a 30 minute drive from our cabin, so he had nothing to worry about.

I was still fighting with the cabin plumbing. By now I had discovered the wonders of pex tubing and shark bite crimp fittings. However I was perplexed by the toilet. I had no idea how to go about connecting the toilet to the drain pipes. Many hours were spent in the Kenai Home Depot, staring at pipes and pipe fittings. There was also mysteries such as vents that need connected. And the problem of connecting the water pump to our water reservoir. Since we had no well, yet, I installed a 50 gallon plastic drum in the bathroom. I glued a 1 inch pex fitting into the bottom, and connected this to the water pump, which came from Harbor Freight.

Eventually I called my buddy, Shannon High, and he walked me through setting up the toilet drain pipes. Of course, it is really easy, after you know how. The next cabin will be a breeze. The day before my parents were arriving, it was pressure city (but the toilet was working). The setup was simple enough, but I couldn't get the hot water heater to work reliability. I knew my parents were the picky type, and would be sure to complain if the shower sprayed them with cold water one minute, and boiling the next, to be followed right away with more cold water.

My first problem with the on demand hot water heater was getting it to light. I had it connected to the propane tank, but it wouldn't light, no how, no way. I took the hot water heater apart, played with the fittings, called tech support. Nothing worked. Then, I got the bright idea to check inside the connector that threads onto the heater. There, nicely packed inside, was a circle of plastic, which blocked the gas flow. With the plastic removed, the heater fired right up.

The toilet was a popular fixture in the cabin. Nothing else was welcomed with such enthusiasm.

With a little training, everyone could have hot showers. The training for folks wanting to take a shower involved a delicate procedure of adjusting knobs on the heater, while hoping the water pump kept up to keep the pressure above 25 psi. If the water pressure dropped, the water would go through the heater slower, creating hotter water, and shrieks could be heard through the whole cabin. So the trick was to not quite open the faucet the entire way, unless you noticed the water pressure dropping. Then you would need to quickly open it the whole way, until the pressure was back up to normal. And if the generator wasn't running, and the batteries dropped too low, they would kick off the inverter and shutdown the water pump. Then your shower was over. Efforts to point out to the family that we were in the Alaskan wilderness, and having any running water should be considered a luxury proved fruitless (and they wanted to hear nothing about "Little House on the Prairie").

June 5th rolled around nice and clear. Josh sent me a text, said "dropped mom and dad off at the airport. Most reluctant travelers ever to go to Alaska" or something like that. Neither of my parents had ever flown before, and they seemed to think most flights ended up crashing into remote, snow capped mountains. My parents (and brother JJ) had a layover in Dallas, Texas. I talked to my dad there, and he seemed in good spirits. His leg kept causing trouble, it would swell unless he propped it up. Other than that, they were somewhat enjoying themselves.

Around 7pm they arrived in Anchorage International Airport. My mom seemed elated and surprised to still be alive. We packed their luggage into the limo, then grabbed supper at the same Denny's we took Josh the evening he arrived. Next, we needed to decided if we should drive down to Anchor Point, about 4 hours away, or hit up a motel in Anchorage. We soon discovered the motels in Anchorage are pretty expensive. Several we checked were almost $200 a night. Then we found a dumpy looking, probably rat infested one for $70 a night. So we booked two rooms, only to find they smelled like a smoking parlor. At that point my parents were so tired they didn't care.

While we were settling into our dumpy little hovel that evening, we heard a commotion outside. We were on the second floor and overlooked a small bar or tavern. A woman of rather questionable looking moral character (the kind the Bible warns you about) was shouting, and appeared to be

Enthusiasm reigns over new throne, Maiden flush proves successful

Submitted on Tue, 05/27/2014

So far since we have arrived in Alaska this year, we have experienced a 5.5 magnitude earthquake, slept within 2 miles of the second largest wildfire in the history of Alaska, complete with evacuation warnings. I also had folks explain to me what to do if the local volcano, Mt. Redoubt erupts. (Mt. Redoubt can be clearly seen directly out our front windows) I was told to keep a pair of panty hose available to put over the cars air cleaner, otherwise your engine gets toasted from the fine ash, which passes right through a normal air filter. I also heard stories from the locals about a grizzly bear taking 11 shots from a .300 Winchester Magnum before expiring, and talked first hand to someone who was charged by a brown bear and shot it 12 times with a .44 magnum, before it ran off. Another fellow I talked to was chased up a tree by a grizzly (despite all these bear stories, we have yet to see one bear in Alaska this year).

So you would think by this time we would be hastily packing our bags for Pa, looking nervously over our shoulders. Not so. I am sitting on my leather couch, picked up cheap, courtesy of craigslist, while listening to rain on the cabin's tin roof. Outside the suburban is quietly rusting, a fire is crackling away in the pot bellied stove. (overnight it gets fairly cold) Irish praise and worship music by Robin Mark is playing on my computer, and I feel quite relaxed. I am very glad for the rain, as this will surely help slow down the wildfires. These fires have been raging around 50 miles from our cabin, not a threat to us, however they have been burning right down the road from our friends house.

So, back to the cabin. It was with great fan fare that today the toilet was installed. Everyone crowded around while I assembled it and ran the pipes, a rather boring process to watch, under normal circumstances. However this heralded the end of trips to the bushes (Not to be confused with Bushes) in the middle of the night. With breathless anticipation I hit the lever, and "whoosh" the toilet flushed, just like a toilet should. Marlene confessed she was a little bit surprised by that. (I'm not sure what she was expecting)

       To celebrate, I brewed a pot of coffee and drank half of it. No more careful, small sips before bed. As I mentioned earlier, we also found 2 leather sofas on craigslist, less than 10 miles from the cabin. We paid a total of $200 for them. We also found a propane refrigerator on craigslist, and our cabin windows.
-Matt

attempting to physically assault some guy in the parking lot. Soon she ran off, fleeing down the street. A few minutes later a police car pulled up, and a police man starting questioning people. Seeing the excitement was over, we went back into our room and tried to sleep.

The next morning we headed south, eager to show my parents the beauty of Alaska. Cruising down the now familiar stretch of Turnagain Arm, the weather was clear and nice. Turnagain Arm is part of Cook Inlet. Driving through there I always look to see if some whales are stranded at low tide. Supposedly sometimes they get stuck there, but I have never seen any. Marlene still doesn't believe me that whales get stuck there.

The day before I did successfully get the toilet to work, so my parents were agreed to at least try sleeping in the cabin. We also by now had purchased a queen sized bed and mattress. With my dad's medical condition, I seriously doubted he wanted to sleep on the floor (actually, I'm not sure he would have wanted to sleep on the floor in the best of health). Shane and JJ slept in the loft, and the girls on the sofa. Marlene and I slept on an air mattress in the second bedroom.

Not wanting to waste a trip, we stopped at WalMart in Kenai for some supplies. Naturally, we wondered over to sporting goods to check out the firearms (Alaskan Walmarts are well stocked with guns). Before I knew what happened, Dad was purchasing a 12 gauge pump shotgun, and some 600 grain bear slugs. I guess he wasn't taking any chances, and I never saw him more than 10 feet from the cabin without it. Soon we were back on the road again. My parents did enjoy the scenery, and had to admit Alaska was "pretty nice." Alan had graciously allowed me to loan his "Rhino" side by side, however I never got around to hauling it down to Anchor Point. So we had to ferry my parents in via the Honda 4 wheeler.

With two extra adults and an additional boy in the cabin, water consumption jumped considerably. Almost every day we were making the 2 mile drive to the river to pump water out. The efficiency of our system was severely lacking, so my dad and I got a brainstorm. Previously I had purchased an upright freezer off of craigslist for $25, and to my surprise, it didn't work. We laid the freezer on it's back, knocked out the shelves, and put in a sheet of plastic. Instant water tank! And that's how we hauled water. One freezer load of water would hold about 70 gallons. The water tank was put on Marlin's trailer, and pulled with the 4 wheeler. It did make the Honda grunt a little, but it worked.

Book about grisly Alaska Bear Attacks

Unfortunately, it wasn't all fun and games in Alaska. Often, work would get in the way. And this presented an interesting paradox. To many people, they would consider building a cabin work. I thought it was fun. Many people would think of tinkering around on a computer as fun, but for me it is work. Now, if I start building cabins all the time, I imagine this would soon reverse itself.

Often over this time I would find myself working late into the night on the computer, trying to catch up with office work. One of our employees, Ken, likes to start working at 4 or 5am. He says "He can't sleep sometimes." Because of the 4 hour time lag between Alaska and Pennsylvania, he would sometimes be starting the day while I was ending it. This would result in interesting conversations on the computer chat.

Having a computer job and sitting around like a slug all week leaves one feeling like they don't really need rest on Sunday. This would result in animated discussions with others about if a "day of rest" was required by scripture. After actually physically working all week, I soon decided I didn't care if a day of rest was required or not, I was going to be taking one!

Electric lights! I hauled these up from Pa, only to discover I could buy them for the nearly the same price in AK. Below you can see the back of our improvised water trailer.

With no required building codes in rural Alaska, it leads to some shortcuts, such as the van septic tank. Another shortcut is the "sand point" well. The basic premise is that you hammer a pipe down into the water table, then pump all the water you want out, laughing at how you save yourself a fortune in well drilling bills.

The water table on our property is at around 14 feet. It is in a layer of sand, which would also act as a filter, resulting in clean water. I decided it wouldn't hurt to try a sand point well out, after Alan Reinford told me about them. Finding the right tools was a bit tricky. I soon found it must not have been a staple for Alaskan living. After calling several plumbing supply stores, I found one that had a well point. This looks like a cone shaped pipe, that threads onto more pipe that you hammer into the ground.

Perhaps our ground was harder than most, or I did something wrong. It took lots of effort to drive it into the ground. Every 4 feet I would thread on another section of pipe, so I could keep driving it further. I kept stripping the threads on the pipe section couplers.

Finally at 14 feet we did hit water. The red tool in the picture below is used for driving pipe into the ground. Unfortunately we did not have any success pumping the water out of the ground. Perhaps I gave up too quickly, but I did end up calling a well driller. But, like most things in Alaska, this didn't happen quickly. So we are still hauling water.

In the picture below you can see the required items for a sand point well. The coupler is on the left, this threads onto your pipe ends. The well point is on the right. In the middle is the driving cap, which goes on the pipe so you don't damage the threads while beating on it. I can see how it would work, maybe I'll try again.

My dad works at driving the sand point well deeper into the ground.

I asked Marlene what she remembers about my parents visit. "Half the time they were here you were hauling water" she said. On our water trips we relished the thought of running into bears. The AR-15 was strapped across the front of the 4 wheeler, I kept a .454 on my belt, and my dad sat on a chair in the trailer wielding his 12 gauge. But, we would have had the same results carrying fly swatters, on those trips. We did often see moose along side the road, but they just watched us drive by, with blank looks on their faces.

One afternoon we decided to all go down to Homer fishing. One of the best places to fish on the spit is "Lands End", located at the end of the spit. The trick is to go when the water is not moving, the hour before and after high tide, or low tide. Other times the fish need to fight the current, so they just wait.

We caught some flounder, I thought they were halibut but later a local fisherman informed us they were not. The Pollock were also biting. I later told someone we caught "Pollocks" and he almost laughed himself senseless. He informed us of the difference between people living in Poland and the fish we were catching.

As we were finished, we noticed a sea otter swimming back and forth. They are very intriguing to watch. We also observed Orca's swimming past, much further out in the sea. This reminded me of the kind hearted people that found an otter covered in oil, gently cleaned it, and tenderly nursed it back to health. Several months, and several thousand dollars later, they released it with great fanfare at the beach. As it swam out to sea, an orca swam by and ate it. Now, this could be an urban legend. However, we know for a fact killer whales eat sea otters. How do we know the rehabilitated sea otters didn't get eaten after they swam out of site?

Shane caught this little flounder (above). Originally we thought it was a Halibut, but we were informed that it was not. The Homer Spit is a narrow strip of land that runs out into the inlet at Homer. Below are some boats docking at the spit. There are also restaurants and small shops along the spit.

It was a little chilly fishing, and the children got tired of it fairly quick. Sometime I want to go on a charter boat, but we were feeling cheap at the time. The best way to catch halibut is from a boat. The biggest halibut are far away from shore. A 20 pound halibut is considered small, big enough for me. They call these "chicken" halibut. Some folks report being able to catch 20 pound halibut from shore, which we tried. But we didn't have any success fishing off the beach.

On the spit we noticed a restaurant advertising half priced halibut dinners. Lacking wisdom we avoided the expensive, quality, halibut restaurant and entered the discount halibut establishment. It was called "Happy Moon Eatery" or something similarly stupid sounding. One bite of the halibut and I knew we had been duped. This wasn't the succulent sea delicacy I knew. To this day I think my parents suspect I am stretching the truth when discussing the merits of eating halibut.

While out in Homer we stopped at a Salvation Army store for my parents to buy souvenirs. My parents are the thrifty type and don't like wasting money at tourist traps. My dad bought a hat that had some kind of outfitters logo on and "Homer, Alaska." My brother JJ managed to find a shirt that said "Alaska" on it for like $2. I'm not sure what my mom got, probably dishes or coffee cups.

After returning to the cabin, we tried our hand at butchering the fish. This didn't go so good. The flounder had a fillet about the size of something you would get off of a hamster, and the Pollock was full of worms. Little, white looking worms that reminded me a lot of maggots. We fried it up anyway (after picking the worms out), but a McDonalds fish sandwich would have been considerably better. To my surprise, my dad consented to just throwing the fish remains in the bushes close to the cabin. I thought he would have wanted to rent a skid loader and bury them several feet deep, with all the bear talk.

Before we knew it, it was time for my parents to head back to Pennsylvania. They flew out on a Saturday evening, and we stayed in Anchorage overnight. My dad left his shotgun at our place, which we nicknamed "Mabel", after his mean step grandmother who ran a liquor store years ago. She was also well known for yelling "call the ambulance! I'm having a heart attack." Only to say a few moments later "it's just gas", followed by further evidence. Truth is stranger than fiction.

My dear mother holding "Mabel" the shotgun. She was only holding this while my dad was tying his shoe. She told me (after much begging) that I could include the picture, but not make it full page or real big. Behind her is "Tall Tree Avenue".

Below we are at the end of the Homer Spit fishing. This is right below "Lands End" at low tide.

With my parents gone, I turned my attention back to the cabin. It still needed flooring finished, insulating, and lots and lots of detail work. We also had another situation looming. We were expecting a baby in August, and we needed to find a midwife. If we did not find one soon, we would be running out of time to return to Pennsylvania to use our previous midwife. I certainly did not want to be helping birth a baby somewhere in the middle of Canada. Yes, you read this correctly, my wife voluntarily braved the wilderness while expecting a baby. Like Marlin says "It's hard not to like a woman like that."

After searching around, the cheapest midwife we could find was $8,000. The hospital in Homer charged around $20,000 for deliveries. It would be far, far cheaper to have the baby in Pennsylvania. I felt terrible not being able to award our new baby an Alaskan birth certificate. Our rental agreement with our old house in Pa had fallen through, so we would be able to use that for the time being. It was a dilemma indeed. To top it off, the baby was due right in the middle of moose season.

A Pennsylvania midwife: $800. An Alaskan midwife: $8,000. That left $7,200 to cover the trip south and back. The moose would have to wait. Even I couldn't justify spending $7,200 on moose hunting, despite all the delicious, healthy, free range meat you get from a moose. Besides, Marlene would look pretty dimly upon me running off into the woods and letting her with a newborn baby.

Before our first Alaskan summer came to a close, with tears in our eyes, we headed south. On the way out we dropped the Suburban off at a local garage, All American Motors. The Suburban had developed some brake problems, which caused the one front tire to lock up, while the other brakes did nothing. This caused some interesting situations. Once, while Marlene was towing Alan Reinford's very nice enclosed trailer, I almost plowed into her from behind with the Suburban. I was not going fast enough to hurt anyone, but it would have caused damage to the trailer, I'm sure. After that incident the Suburban stayed mostly parked (I still used it to pull trailers in and out our muddy lane).

I knew All American Motors was a good garage, by the size of the bears they had on display. Anybody that shoots bears that big can't be all bad. Norm, the owner said it took "11 shots from a .375 H&H magnum while on snow shoes. It was exciting." I didn't doubt that. Shane is standing beside a mount of this bear, pictured on the next page.

PLEASE DO NOT
FEED OR TOUCH
BEARS

Here are some pictures of the cabin, and how far along we are at this point in time. With Tyvek on, the cabin fits right into the landscape.

I couldn't help but feel a little good about our modest cabin we built from scratch. Alan Reinford donated the moose antlers to our cause.

Desiree standing in the door way of the one bedroom. Shane attempts to look like a Viking, but I doubt they had such huge antlers on their helmets.

Heading south to have a baby-Chapter 11

Oddly, Marlene seemed happy to be going south. Soon we encountered a problem. Just outside of Sterling, on our way to Pa, we got pulled over by the police. I thought this may have had something to do with the fact Kallia was hanging over the divider in the console. But the officer didn't even mention that. Rather, he wondered if I had straight pipes on the limo. "No" I replied, "they are flowmasters." He seemed satisfied with this answer, then asked for my insurance card. I pulled out a paper the agent in Alaska had given me. "This won't work, you need something else" he told me. That was all I had, so he told me he would have to write a ticket. "Don't worry though" he said, "Just bring your insurance card to the station before 30 days are up and we'll throw out the ticket." I informed him we were actually heading out of Alaska, and wouldn't be back until more than 30 days.

"Just take your insurance card to the state police in Pa", he told me. "They will know what to do, or even a Canadian Mountie." Ok, I really didn't believe the Canadian Mounties would know how to cancel out an Alaskan traffic citation, but who was I to argue. But when I looked at the citation, the fine was $1,000 and I would lose my new Alaskan drivers license for several months. I decided I would certainly be looking into it.

We saw quite a few bears on our way down the Alcan highway, more than any other trip. Several grizzlies and several black bears.

These crazy mountain goats acted half tame. We could almost walk right up to them, and this is in the middle of nowhere.

We made record time on the trip to Pennsylvania. It took us 5.5 days to drive 4,400 miles. That was with 5 children in the car. We only stopped to sleep for the night once, the rest of the time we would just change drivers. Occasionally we would take naps at rest areas. We were pretty grumpy by the time we pulled into Middleburg, Pa. Our rental agreement for the house in Pa had fallen though, so we decided we might as well stay there to have the baby.

I felt homesick immediately upon leaving Alaska. It just seemed wrong to leave our new home state so quickly. We would be back as fast as I could help it.

August 21 we welcomed Mary Kate into the world. We felt blessed and excited to have another member of the family. The midwife cautioned us against driving such a long distance with a new baby and mom, and I agreed she was probably right. Pennsylvania is a nice state, it wasn't quite like being stuck in North Korea. The websites we manage kept me busy as well, so time went by quickly.

For years I had mistakenly assumed 4 wheelers were frivolous toys, and secretly questioned the wisdom of folks who had them. Our stay in Alaska had opened my eyes. I realized if you live in a long, very muddy lane, and plan on hauling supplies and materials in and out the lane, then you really need a four wheeler. There were also a hundred other useful things they could do. Plow snow, pull farming implements, drag dead moose out of the woods, pull vehicles out of ditches, the list just goes on and on. Considering our plan to build rental cabins, it just seemed foolish to brave the wilderness without reliable equipment.

I started considering our return trip to Alaska. Folks had questioned my wisdom on driving old, high mileage vehicles, pointing out that even Larry Burkett advised replacing equipment at some point. I decided they were right, so I bought a new four wheeler. After all, in Alaska, a 4 wheeler is your main mode of transportation. Marlin had wanted his back, and it wouldn't be wise to haul children around the wilderness in old, used modes of transportation. After all, if a car breaks down, you're probably alongside a road. If your 4 wheeler breaks down, you might be in the middle of the wilderness. Hauling the 4 wheeler in a trailer behind our van on the way to Alaska, it would also serve as a type of lifeboat. If the van breaks down, we would just drive the 4 wheeler to the next town and summon help.

Mary Kate Snader was born on August 21 at 8:07am, 8 pounds 1 oz, 21 inches long. The whole family was delighted to meet her. I was a little worried about getting her paperwork in time to go back to Alaska (birth certificate, etc) but that all went without a hitch.

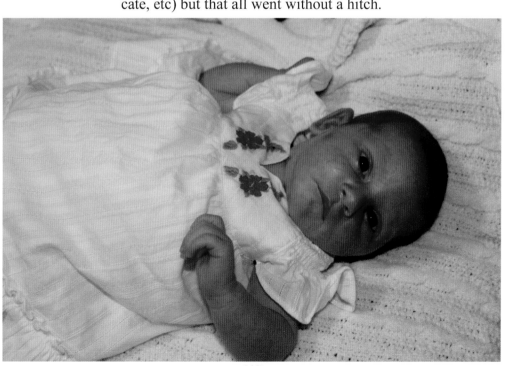

The children liked the 4 wheeler even better than I did. Not wanting to come across as extravagant, I purchased one with a 700 cc engine. It has plenty of power, but maybe some day I'll get a model with 1,000 cc. I purchased this form Millers Turf & Trail near Mifflinburg, Pa. It has done well for us, and logged many hours since in Alaska, without incident.

Thieves strike the cabin! - Chapter 12

We were not going to be in Alaska for a month or more, so I asked my brother if he would want to fly up and work on the cabin. Children living in a construction zone makes for some interesting moments and I thought they might get a lot more work done with us gone. Ira, a fellow from church also decided to fly up with Josh. Ira was an authentic carpenter, and a bit of a perfectionist. I hoped Josh wouldn't drive him insane. Originally Josh and Ira planned to drive the limo up, but time restraints dictated otherwise.

September 4th was the scheduled day of Josh and Ira's departure. Marlene and I ran them to the Philadelphia airport. I was a little nervous Ira would think our setup in Alaska was horrid, and want to just torch it. He never did tell me what he thought of the cabin, but he hinted to Josh that he found the Suburban unsatisfactory, after they picked it up at the garage. "I bet $50 this thing won't even last till this day is over" he told Josh. Josh, of course disagreed. But, not being a betting man, he wouldn't put money on it (Josh later admitted that he wasn't sure it was last the day either). Ira also told Josh "I thought Matt was normal, and what kind of wife does he have?" I was flattered that Ira apparently thought of me as above average, and was pleased that he seemed to think I chose a good wife.

When Josh and Ira arrived at the cabin it looked like a mess. He called me and said he was surprised how messy I left it. That puzzled me, because I thought we had cleaned up pretty nice, and Josh was a bachelor. "Look around" I told him. "Someone else must have been in there." Sure enough, we found a note some lawless breaking and enterers had left. They claimed they were out picking berries, got lost, and found our inviting cabin. After this I put no trespassing signs every where, so at least it won't look as inviting. The term "berry picker" soon became used as an insult in our vocabulary.

When I complained to my neighbor about this, he said someone broke into his house, which is actually a shipping container, and stole his favorite pistol. And, he said, "he didn't even get a note out of it." I guess I do have a lot to be thankful for. Our intruders must not have been malicious, as they left 600 rounds of .223 ammo untouched. The guns were not there, I locked them up at a friends place. What is very puzzling though, is that they nailed a bathroom cabinet to the kitchen wall. Perhaps they thought they would help out with the cabin construction, and were too inept and stupid to realize that was not helpful. It is also worth noting it was not cold out when this happened.

Sincerely Owners,
   We are so grateful you have such a inviting place. We've been very poor and lost on our way and we are so happy you were still with us for dinner the kids we are so hungry

Another problem presented itself with Josh and Ira in Alaska. Our awful "lane" had again turned to a soupy mess, and each trip in and out represented a serious risk of getting stuck. Marlin was using his four wheeler for hunting, or probably was, as it was approaching moose season. Alan was definitely using his for moose hunting. So, I reluctantly called the Honda dealer and ordered a new Foreman 500 4x4 four wheeler. Being the frugal type, I selected a "bare bones" model. This machine is great, except for one thing, I hate the foot shifter. Next time I am going to get a shifter on the handle bars. My boot is to big to fit in it right, so switching gears is a pain. Note: You don't want to buy used 4 wheelers in Alaska, they are run hard up there.

The reason I decided on a Honda was the Polaris dealer was out of their 800's (moose season cleaned out the inventory), and I had been very impressed with Marlin's Honda. Before this year, all the 4 wheelers I had used broke down about every 20 minutes. So I was under the impression you couldn't even run a full tank of gas through one without needing repairs. Marlin's 4 wheeler proved this was not true.

When Josh and Ira picked up the 4 wheeler at Ron's Honda Center in Soldotna, the fellow helping them load it remarked "your brother should spend more money on vehicles and less on four wheelers." Sorry, but I don't take financial advice from ATV dealers. Sounds risky.

Josh texted me a picture of the new four wheeler on the trailer. I was a bit horrified with their strapping arrangements. I had a new $7,200 machine hanging by a thread, it seemed. I called Josh, only to find they were wondering around in Home Depot. Concerned that someone might help themselves to my new 4 wheeler in the parking lot, held on by a thread, Josh responded "Ira thought it would be ok." I encouraged them to buy some more straps and make sure no one stole the four wheeler. The next phone call was to my insurance agent.

Despite Josh and Ira's questionable hauling practices, the Honda made it safely back to Anchor Point. I breathed a sigh of relief. Josh and Ira turned out to be much better at construction than hauling. They would send me periodic updates, along with photos of moose they saw outside the cabin. This did little to make me feel happy to be stuck back in Pa. One consolation, it rained almost every day they were there.

Even I couldn't help but be impressed when Josh sent me the photo of the new 4 wheeler at the Honda dealer. Josh vainly attempts to hide his pride as he poses in front of my Suburban. He also is modeling the latest trend in vintage Alaskan attire, "flannel".

This is the same trailer that Ken hauled to Colorado. You can see it seems to have aged considerably since then. Josh reported getting a flat tire on the way back to Anchor Point with the trailer. As you can see in the picture below, there are only two frayed little straps holding the 4 wheeler on the trailer, hence my nervousness...

Moose right outside our cabin window

One day Josh emailed me and asked when his flight was returning. I sent him the date and time, and got an unusual response. "That won't work" he said. "I have plans that day. I thought the flight was returning 8 hours sooner." This is from a guy that went to the airport on the wrong day last time. "Ok", I responded. "I'll see if I can change the tickets."

The ticket agent didn't seem to like a change in plans. She informed me that it would cost $400 to change the ticket. "Wow", I thought. "Forget that." So I emailed Josh and told him what happened. "Ok", he said, "I'll change my plans." About an hour later he responded and said "I'll just pay the $400 and fly back a day sooner." This is from a guy that drives an old car he paid $600 for. That of course is a fine habit (the old car), but not typical behavior of someone throwing $400 out the window to get home a few hours earlier.

A suspicion began to grow in the back of my mind. There was only one reason a cheapskate bachelor would throw caution and money to the wind. There could be only one force on earth capable of making him act so irrationally (besides earthquakes and hurricanes, possibly). Then he emailed me again, "Ok, I admit it, I have a date with a beautiful woman." His first date ever, actually. At least that I am aware of. The plane tickets were re-scheduled.

Cabinets that the parasitic "berry pickers" nailed to the wall, as well as the mess they made in the sink.

Below you can see the progress Josh and Ira made on the ceiling. They insisted on trimming the ceiling, which I thought was unnecessary. However after they were done I was glad I listened to Ira's construction expertise. Josh said they would have "Just done it anyway" had I told them not to.

Here the ceiling is all finished out! I must admit I liked the way it looked with trim much better. Below they are sanding the floor down, getting it ready for linoleum. You can see the barrel I use for a water reservoir on the right, and my handy water pump. The washer will go right beside the water pump on the left.

Josh and Ira also finished the tongue and groove paneling in the cabin, and rehung my kitchen cabinets. Every day or two they would email me updates on the cabin finishing, which I would eagerly look for. Occasionally Josh would casually make statements that made me a little nervous, like "did you know the 4 wheeler can go 55 mph?" Or "the suburban is really leaking transmission fluid."

Josh sent me a picture the one day of the 4 wheeler stuck in the mud. I was slightly worried the engine would get water in it, or some other bad thing would happen, but Josh assured me it was tough. Below you can see the batteries and invertor setup after Josh and Ira cleaned up and paneled the bathroom. I thought the results of their work was rather impressive. Electricians will admire my handiwork at the breaker box. Sorry, I don't make house calls.

That sad day came when Josh and Ira were planning to leave Anchor Point. Although neither Josh or Ira seemed very tore up about it. Their plans were to drive up to Denali State Park, do some sightseeing for a day or two, then fly back into the armpit of civilization. Up until now they had managed to avoid getting stuck in the lane. But on the last day, on the last trip out, the Suburban had other plans. It ground to a halt halfway out the lane, and would not budge. Josh called me, sounding a bit agitated. "The Suburban is stuck" he said. I offered him practical advice, like "push on it while Ira floors the throttle", but nothing worked. It wouldn't budge. "Do your best", I told him.

An hour and half went past, and I assumed they must have gotten un-stuck. Then I got another phone call. I don't remember what Josh said, but words were not needed to determine he was having a bad day. They had missed their free ride to Anchorage, and were still stuck in the mud. I was 4,000 miles away, so my hands were a bit tied. "Call Alan or Marlin" I suggested. Indeed, Alan came to the rescue and hauled them up to his place. They stayed there overnight, then grabbed a flight from Kenai to Anchorage, where they had a car waiting. The Suburban stayed safely lodged in the driveway until I returned and pushed it out with a skid loader.

Plans were to store the 4 wheeler at Alan's or Marlin's, just in case thieving berry pickers would show up again. But with the change of plans with the Suburban, I called neighbor Ron and asked if he would babysit the four wheeler for a few weeks until I got back. He very readily agreed, and promptly picked it up, fixing that problem. At this point I didn't know Ron very well, but figured he couldn't be any worse than a wondering, scaveng-ing, all things good hating berry picker (I later discovered Ron was a very decent sort, not at all like a berry picker).

In Denali they couldn't find a motel vacancy, so they ended up sleep-ing in the pickup truck. A day or two later we picked them up at Philadelphia International Airport. They had calmed down by then, and were able to talk conversely. Ira also seemed giddy with excitement to be back, which made me wonder if he had similar plans as Josh. It was hard to imagine being glad to leave Alaska, but I guess we need folks like that so Alaska doesn't get crowded.

Josh and Ira discovered my little 2000 watt Honda generator was not big enough to run the air compressor. So they picked up this rustic looking "Subaru" generator at a local pawn shop for $150. Below are some more moose calves, this picture was also taken close to our cabin. Around them you can see "Fireweed", which is rather pretty.

How to Drive to Alaska for Free!

Chapter 13

If your hoping to drive to Alaska, but you can't bring yourself to spend the money, this tip is for you! This tip may well be worth the (quite modest) purchase price of this book. I was told by several Alaskans that I should bring an enclosed trailer up and sell it, which would generate enough profit to pay for the gas. Always on the lookout to save money (I consider myself quite frugal), I decided this was worth a try. They also told me the larger the trailer, the more profit.

I ordered a new enclosed trailer from a company in Georgia that I thought was reasonably priced. It was brand new, 24 feet long, with two 5400 pound axles, radial tires, only $5,200. It also had a side door and window. We decided to use this for a camper on the return trip to Alaska. This idea sounded great in theory, but was a little lacking in real life. My brother in law accused me of gravitating between two extremes with my trailer buying habits.

To keep the trailer warm I mounted a propane wall heater in it. I also attempted to connect a water tank to an on demand hot water heater, but this proved to be a failure. It would have worked fine, but some of our couplers sprouted leaks and water ran all over the floor. Not wanting to waste cargo space I purchased two 275 gallon water tanks to take along up. There was also a snowmobile, or "snowmachine" rather, that I traded my old plow truck for. It was an Arctic Cat 800, perfect for tearing up the Alaskan powder. There was room for the new four wheeler too. The trailer wouldn't have been complete without some bunk bed cots. These turned out to be a great idea, and the children loved the novelty of it.

Concerned about the possibility of driving through snow on the Alcan, I ordered some new tires for our van. We would be driving the van, as the limo could not pull such a huge trailer. It was sad indeed to leave the limo behind, but it would see Alaska again. To prevent our van suspension from sagging I installed some air bags. These worked out quite well and help stabilize it. We didn't leave for Alaska until early October. Ordering a trailer in Georgia and having to go pick it up didn't speed up the process. But finally, we were on the way back to our new home state.

I was slightly startled how big this trailer actually was when I picked it up. But the van pulled it without hesitation. Plenty of room for all kinds of things!

We left Middleburg, Pa, on a Sunday afternoon after church. It was a nice day, which was good, as I had to throw a few things in the trailer yet. These "few things" turned into several hours. I was beginning to sense hostility in Marlene by the time we hit the road. I tried to tell her that, I being the leader of the household, had many important things to tend to that she didn't have to worry about. She seemed to have other opinions about the late start that didn't involve quality leadership skills.

The van was performing well, except for some horrible shifting. I had to hit the throttle hard, then let off, then hit it again, in order to coax it to shift. I figured this was due to the weight in the trailer, and didn't pay it any mind. After all, we had just installed a new Jasper transmission in it a few months before. The van and trailer usually did pretty well on the highway. It drove much better than the van I bought for $400 and drove to Mexico (that van wouldn't go over 55mph with the trailer). The fuel mileage was a little less than desirable though. I got 9 mpg on most tanks.

This time the trailer didn't blow tires or start on fire. It was quite re-freshing. It was a little tricky getting used to pulling the trailer, as it stuck out about half a foot on either side of the van. This wasn't a big problem, except navigating "cattle chutes." Those one lane construction zones with concrete barriers put as close together as possible. On several occasions I thought the pieces would fly, but we made it without incident.

Below you can see some of our humble trailer accommodations. Some well meaning people suggested this wall mounted heater would either A. Start the trailer on fire and burn us alive. Or B. Kill us all in our sleep. I'm happy to report neither happened, and it actually worked flawlessly. We did let the trailer vent and window open a little when sleeping in it, just in case.

On the wall you can also see our smaller on demand hot water heater. This I brought along in an attempt to tame our wild hot water heater that was in our cabin, but I found later that the problem was with the cabin water pres-sure tank. You can see our "double bunk" cots in the picture. Despite the cot weight ratings of 300 pounds, Marlene insisted I sleep on the bottom bunk. And of course, I never drove while people slept in the trailer.

We discovered we were pushing the close of camping season. All the campgrounds we stopped at were open, although we stopped at one on the last day of the season. That particular campground had a maintenance man with an attitude. First he gave me a hard time for pulling into the parking spot, instead of backing in. It was after 8pm when we arrived, and the campground was deserted. It was also muddy, cold and raining. I decided there was no need to back in, and this seemed to upset the fellow. Next, he told me I couldn't use the shower in the bathroom. The office had told me I could. He explained that the bathrooms had been repainted, and apparently the paint need more time to dry because the doors were still taped shut (according to the maintenance man).

The solution was simple, I took the tape off the doors. Then I found the maintenance man and told him "this stall doesn't have tape on it, may I take a shower." He said to go ahead. Taking a warm shower is a big deal when you have been driving for a few days without one, especially when your paying full price to park there anyway. Besides, the paint seemed quite cured in the stall, and the office told me "the showers are open."

We usually cross into Canada from North Dakota, at a small crossing called "North Portal." A few hours from the border we stopped at a Culvers, our favorite fast food restaurant. This stop turned into a mini disaster. Standing in line to order, Samantha decided to stop standing up, and let her knees buckle. She was holding onto Marlene's hand, and her sudden drop caused her arm to twist. This must have popped it out of joint, and she was inconsolable. At the same time, Marlene dropped Mary Kate's car seat on the ground, and she started crying loudly.

I took the children back to a corner table while Marlene waited on the food. The children finally calmed down a bit, and it seemed like half the restaurant was staring at us. Samantha would periodically cry, so Marlene went out to the van with her. Mary Kate decided to cry also, and finally we all went out to the van. There we were faced with a dilemma: It was late evening, nothing was open, and it seemed Samantha's arm was out of place. We prayed about it, and I pulled gently on Samantha's arm. I heard a "pop", and she immediately started crying less. Soon it was obvious it did not hurt anymore. Praising the Lord, we headed "north" again.

A day earlier in Minnesota, we were busted for the children not having seatbelts. This was due to our back seat having been "jerry rigged" into the van. My apologies to anyone named Jerry. Our van from the factory was only an 8 passenger. Someone stuck another seat in, which was a fantastic idea, but they forgot to include seat belts. Naturally the children like sitting where they shouldn't. Also due to the fact they fight a lot (imagine that) we had them separated as far apart as we could in all the seats.

I had forgotten about this seat belt issue, until I was sitting at a red light somewhere in Minnesota. Suddenly I heard someone knocking on the back windows and shouting. "What in the world" I thought. Here it was a policeman. "Your children are not strapped in!" he said sternly. I mentally made a note to get darker tint on the van windows. At first I had no idea what he was talking about, and a bit taken aback, and must have looked it, because he didn't say much more but told me to pull over beside the road.

After I pulled over, another policeman came up and explained that he was going to give me a ticket for the children not having seatbelts. Having by now remembered our seatbelt issue with the back seat, I knew that I was in fact at fault. Not much to say when it is your fault. He went on to explain that he could give me a $100 ticket for every children not strapped in, which was the 3 in the back. I mentally prepared myself for a donation of $300 to Minnesota's finest. "But" the officer continued, "I'll just give you a ticket for one child and two warnings." Wow! Maybe they do that sort of thing on purpose so you don't argue-but I was happy about that.

I was also questioned if I was a resident of Minnesota, and if I had a van full of guns. No on all accounts. He then asked if I had any questions. "Yes" I replied. "Is it true you don't need seat belts in a motor home?" The officer said, "Yes, that is correct. Motor homes do not require seat belts for the passengers, only the front 2 seats." I made a mental note to get a cheap motorhome sometime soon.

So we were off again. I didn't explain to the officer that the van did not have seatbelts on those seats, and he didn't bother checking, much to my relief. I guess we could always use ratchet straps. To all of you wringing your hands about my breaking the law, not to worry, I later remedied the situation. I purchased a 21 year old motorhome. But that's for another book.

It was around 2am that we got to the border. Last time I came through pulling a trailer they about strip searched us, so I was expecting a lot of horsing around. Most of the children were sleeping. As I pulled up, the guard started asking the usual questions, "where are you going?", "why?", "when was the last time you came through here?", etc. Then he asked me if I owned any pistols. "Yes", I replied, "but not along with me." I told him I did have some ammunition along, in the trailer. He asked "Is that for your pistols in the trailer?" "No, no pistols in the trailer" I told him. This went round and round for a minute. I finally told the guard I would open the trailer up and he could have a look. At that, he handed me my passports back, and told me to "enjoy our trip", we were cleared for entry. That was the quickest border crossing ever.

The drive through Canada was breath taking, as usual. Most folks that drive to Alaska do it in the summer. The scenery is incredible then, as well. But to be a well rounded individual you really need to also drive the Alcan highway when there is snow on the ground. It is very beautiful. Fortunately the drive was uneventful, except for our crazy shifting transmission. We had to go slow up mountains, if you lugged it to hard it would simply downshift and nearly blow the engine up.

Crossing back into Alaska was even easier than getting into Canada. I was worried about my "snowmachine", because I didn't have a title for it. The guard didn't even ask what was in the trailer, except if it was "personal items." This crossing took even less time than coming into Canada. It was very exciting to be back in Alaska!

The first stop was at Marlins. I brought some trailer parts along for him, then on to the Reinford's to pickup our guns. It was cold out, and I wasn't in the mood for a bear to rip off my coat. Then it was on to Anchor Point, where our cabin awaited. When we arrived, the first thing to greet us was the Suburban, still stuck in the lane. I tried the key, and it fired right up! Not bad for a $20 "junk" battery and a $300 rig.

The cabin looked fine. I was worried more berry pickers would come back and move in, but that was not the case. Josh had put up about a dozen "No Trespassing" signs. Perhaps that had scared them off, or maybe they had stayed away for good. I was tempted to put up signs that said "Leave while your able", a favorite quote of my esteemed great uncle Wandon Deihm. He would say this to trespassers, while pointing an old rusty gun at them.

Our family has nothing but the greatest regards for dear great uncle Wandon (he was not related to the step great grandmother who ran the liquor store). He was a bit of an odd bird though. I only met him once, while I was very young, before he passed away. That particular time he was trying to give away a dead raccoon. It was on his porch for awhile, but had been frozen so it was "still good." He lived in the Welsh Mountains in an old farmhouse.

After he passed away, there were reports of strange things found in his house. The most notable were dead cats found in the kitchen cabinets. The strangest thing about these cats was the fact they obviously had been dead for many years. Simple mathematical calculations left one to realize that dear Uncle Wandon had been living for a long time with dead cats in his cupboards. It probably goes without saying that he was a bachelor.

Another relative, my great grandfather Hahn, was known for driving his Model T Ford through the front doors of the Adamstown, PA hat factory. This earned him a stay in the local prison, where he got to know the guards and inmates so well he hated to leave after his sentence was over. There were also rumors that he had counterfeit lead quarters. I'm assuming back then 25 cents went further than it does today.

A week or two after arriving back in Alaska, I was driving the van down the Sterling Highway towards Homer. I forget why I was heading that way, but suddenly the van acted like I was in neutral. Coasting to the side of the road, I got out and looked underneath. I didn't see any ATF fluid spraying, and no tell tail signs of smoke. Feeling a bit disgruntled I called Jasper and let them know I wasn't impressed with their transmission. They told me to get the van towed to the local Jasper dealer, which also happened to be the garage we already used, "All American Motors." I was happy to hear this, as I'm always nervous when dealing with a new garage.

Soon a rollback came and picked us up. I had State Farm trip insurance, so they covered the towing bill. The rollback dropped me off at the end of Tall Tree Ave, but wouldn't take me the 4 miles to our lane. So me and Shane decided we'll just have to walk. It was a nice day, and a pleasant day for a walk. Suddenly I realized that I foolishly left the cabin unarmed that morning. Here I was, walking down the middle of nowhere in Alaska, with nothing but a stick. "Oh well" I thought. "What are the chances of seeing a bear today anyway?"

We hadn't walked long until one of our neighbors came along and gave us a lift. He took us in the lane 2 miles, until his road turned off. Grateful for the lift, we hoofed it the rest of the way. Almost at our lane, we met our other neighbor, Ron, coming up the road. Ron stopped and chatted for a little, then suddenly asked "what are you guys doing, just walking down the road out there?" I explained our van breaking down, but assured him it was under warranty and we would be fine. Before he left, Ron gave us his Ruger .22 rifle to borrow. "You'll need this to shoot spruce chickens", he said. Gotta love a neighbor like Ron!

With the van broke down, we were left with the Suburban, which was still firmly stuck in the mud. Wanting a skid loader for some other work about the property, I called around to see if I could find one to rent. Marlin said he would let me use his, for a modest fee. So he dropped it off, and I promptly used it to push the Suburban out of the mud. The Suburban's rear doors stopped latching after I pushed it out. Perhaps just driving into it with the bucket wasn't the best way to dislodge it.. I did notice bits of trash falling out of the rear quarter panels. Upon investigation I noticed they appeared to be rusted completely out. I'll have to make sure not to let the children sit back there, or they might fall out.

Van selects "Benedict Arnold" as role model, Suburban is old reliable

Submitted on Fri, 10/24/2014 - 9:57am

Yesterday while driving down the Sterling Highway towards Homer, the van suddenly acted like it shifted into neutral. However, it was still in overdrive, but every gear acted like neutral. I admit this is a fuel saver, but highly inconvenient, to say the least. So there wasn't much to do besides call a rollback, while resisting the urge to label the van a number of ungodly things.

The tranny is under warranty, thankfully. It had been replaced about 2 months ago, and the towing bill is covered by State Farm insurance. (despite all those witty gecko ads, I still like State Farm better, after all I'm not running a zoo)

At the garage, Shane and I did get to see a mount of one of the largest brown bears shot in Alaska. It was huge, I'll grab a picture of it next time we are there. Norm, the owner of the garage, said he had to shoot it 11 times with a .375 H&H magnum rifle. I asked him if that was an exciting time. "Yes, especially while wearing snowshoes" was his reply.

So, we are not without a vehicle. I took our rented skidloader and used it to push the suburban out of it's storage spot on the lane. Unfortunately, the suburban shakes like a maniac while cruising at highway speeds. Also a negative is the fact that half the family refuses to be seen it, afraid they will get donations of food and other goods, or tips on the best local homeless shelters, perhaps.

Maybe while the van gets fixed, I'll see if I can find a slightly more expensive, less rusty vehicle to buy. (cheap of course)

Oh, and my good neighbor Ron discovered I did not have a .22 to hunt spruce chickens with. (he thought an AR-15 or .454 would be overkill) So he promptly came over with a Rugar 10-22 .22 Long Rifle for me to use. How can you not enjoy living in Alaska with a neighbor like him. (he also jump started my vehicle the other day)

Have a good day, don't forget to give your mechanic a hug.

Matt

Marlene was concerned about having a washer installed in the cabin. I agreed that was important, as I also hate sitting around laundromats. We purchased a washer in Soldotna, but how to get it in the lane? The Suburban was still as stuck as ever (this was before I pulled the Suburban out), and I didn't want to risk trying to take the van in. Looking at my 4 wheeler, I noticed the rack limit was 250 pounds. Then it hit me, a washer doesn't weigh more than that! So I strapped it on the 4 wheeler and hauled it in the lane that way. It actually worked out very well. And, more importantly, the washer worked after I hooked it up, despite the ride in.

One evening we ran into a small tragedy. Our Honda generator quit working. A normal, seasoned Alaskan would just chuckle and pull out his spare generator. I did have a spare generator, but it was still in Soldotna, at Alan's place. It was that ancient looking model that Josh and Ira had picked up at a pawn shop for $150. I had a real dilemma. Our battery bank only had 2 batteries connected, right then. They were both half dead. There was no way we would have enough electric to run the lights, refrigerator and who knows what else until morning when the sun came up and the solar panels kicked in. As shocking as it sounds, Marlene wasn't quite keen on the idea of sitting around in the dark, with the food slowly going to waste.

Worried about our marriage, I called Ron and ask him if he had a spare generator I could borrow. "Come on down, maybe we can get yours fixed up" he said. Shane and I ran the Honda generator down to Ron's, while riding the Honda 4 wheeler. While at Ron's I learned a lot about the little Honda generators. Ron also is a fan of Stihl Chainsaws. I am too, I have 3 of them.

Our efforts to get the little Honda generator working were fruitless. It was evident that sand had gotten into the gas tank and clogged up the carburetor. But, Ron did have a spare I could borrow. Very thankful, I let him know my appreciation, and back to the cabin we went. I did have extra batteries and solar panels along, but they were not hooked up yet. I decided these needed to be installed, asap. An adequate battery bank and solar panel combination would have made the generator breakdown a non issue.

The Suburban actually did good, for awhile. I ran it up to Soldotna the one day, after which the trailer fell apart. There was also the pizza incident, caused one evening by a flat tire. You can read about those sordid events in the included blog entries. Soon afterwards, the Suburban left me sit. I was really getting my money out of the trip insurance. Thankfully, we broke down close to a cheap van that was for sale. This solved our problem in the short term, but this nice van I picked up didn't have rear passenger seats.

That weekend the Suburban still had a flat tire, I had no way to go get a spare, and our "good" van was in the garage getting another transmission. I had not had the fore sight to purchase a 3rd spare vehicle. You might suggest just driving the four wheeler to town and getting the tire fixed. Good idea, but everything closes on Saturday in Anchor Point. I remember Marlin had said something about him having a spare van.

We decided that it would be a good idea to have at least one vehicle around that had enough seats for everyone. I called Marlin, and he confirmed his van was still available. Dale, Marlin's son, and his daughter Judy ran the van down to us. I owe them a big thank you for doing that, as it is over an hour drive from their place in Sterling to Anchor Point.

It was around this time I started having problems with our water supply. The temperatures would go below freezing over night, but then warm up during the day. Hauling water, up until this point, proved remarkably easy. We would just drive the 4 wheeler down to the creek, with the 275 gallon water tank on the trailer. I had a little 12 volt electric pump from Harbor Freight, which I would use to pump water from the creek into the tank. Then I would drive back to the cabin, and pump the water into the tank inside the cabin. One day I took one of the 275 gallon tanks up to the Reinford's and filled it up at their place. I'll let you read the blog entry on that.

This worked very well, until I started having problems with the water freezing. The one evening I hooked everything up, turned it on, and went inside the cabin. About 20 minutes later I came out to check on the pump. There were little wisps of smoke coming off of it, and it was making a terrible, high pitched racket. The water had frozen in the garden hose, and the pump over heated. The pump never worked again.

Eventually I discovered a solution to our unstable, boil, freeze and scream water heater. The pressure switch gave out on the water pump, causing it to run nonstop. This made a constant, steady stream of water pressure. The water heater worked flawlessly! All I needed was a decent pressure tank, and we would be in business.

Some more photos of the 4 wheelers. Below, Marlin's fine van is on the left, our fine van on the right. Despite being less than a decade old, Marlin's van showed an attitude as well.

Another problem in our meticulous plumbing design was the water tanks themselves. I had added a second 50 gallon tank, doubling our in cabin water supply to a total of 100 gallons. I did this shortly after installing the washer, because I found out washers use lots of water. The issue was the connection between the 2 tanks and the barrels. I simply drilled holes in the tanks, and forced a brass fitting in, and dumped silicone all over it. This worked for awhile, but then it started dripping. And dripping. After awhile the bathroom floor was always wet. With 5 children in the cabin this was especially unnerving, because you could never quite be sure if that was water on the floor, or something else (the water tanks were beside the toilet). I also was worried I would undo Josh and Ira's hard work with the tasteful flooring they installed.

All these problems came to head, naturally, on a late Saturday afternoon. That meant no running water to get ready for church in the morning. Coupled with the fact the ride to church started with packing all the children out the muddy lane on a four wheeler, Sunday mornings were already a bit complicated. I had all the parts to make the setup work, so I stayed up rather late trying to assemble them. I installed a new pressure tank from Home Depot, a monstrous 40 gallon one because they were sold out of everything else. I carefully took all the plastic tank fittings apart and used a more expensive silicone.

After carefully waiting hours for the silicone to dry, I was ready to pump this system full of water. I had already toasted one pump, but I did have a second one. Alaska teaches you pretty quickly to have spares for everything. But, this turned out to be a failure. The temperatures were above freezing earlier in the evening, but till I got everything ready, the lines were froze up again. The water tank on the trailer was still not frozen, because a hundred gallons or so of water stays above freezing for a long time. Tired and disgusted, I went to bed. I did have some water inside the cabin that I dumped into the tanks, which at least let us have running water again.

We did get to church Sunday morning, despite all these problems. Marlene did a great job having the children presentable, although she did drop some hints about the convenience of running water. I must admit she is a patient lady (I don't mean like a mental patient, either).

Monday I noticed more water all over the bathroom floor. By this time Marlene had nothing positive to say about my plumbing skills. The good news is the water barrels were not leaking anymore, but water was coming from the pressure tank connections, and the water pump connections. I had not installed a way to drain the system properly, so taking the fittings apart meant large amounts of water everywhere. That silicone tape is tricky stuff to master. So I called my buddy, Shannon High, and ask him what real plumbers did. Shannon recommend using the paste on the pipe threads, and the plumber tape. That did the trick. No more water everywhere.

With the plumbing actually working right, it was time to tackle the electrical issues. After hooking up the new batteries and panels, which you can read about in the included blog entry, the cabin was almost normal to live in. No longer did the invertor voltage alarm start bellowing in the middle of the night. For the most part, the water actually came out of the faucets (I still have some trouble with the bathroom sink). In the spring of 2015 or early summer we want to get a well drilled, which will go a great deal towards simplifying things.

Antlers make a great rack to hang clothes. Below: Desiree and Kallia like playing in the loft.

Trailer blows last tire, collapses and joins the van club

Submitted on Sat, 10/25/2014 - 11:52am

Yesterday was one of those days that made me realize that while Alaska is indeed a paradise, heaven will be a better place. It all started out in the morning, I decided I wanted to make a "quick" trip to Soldotna to get some building supplies and a new water pump, and swing in at the Reinfords to fill my water tank. After that, I would take our cabin fever stricken family out to Roscoes Pizza. Our old water pump, which has a tiny built in pressure tank, has a habit of making folks taking a shower scream and shout (the pressure fluctuations mess with the on demand water heater, causing wild extremes in water temperature).

When I went to leave, I discovered the trailer lights didn't work, so I had to wait until sunrise. On the way out the lane, the trailer bed decide to fall off the frame, because the bolts in the front fell out. So I quickly ran back to the cabin, and got more bolts to stick in it. After finally getting on the Sterling Highway, I realized the license plate for the trailer was missing. I remembered Shane telling me that he had seen it laying in the weeds. Oh well, I thought, we'll just hope for the best.

Home Depot only had 40 gallon pressure tanks in stock, which for our cabin is like hunting rabbits with a 10 gauge, however I decided that would have to work (after each stop the suburban delightfully started up). So after loading up on all the supplies, I headed back through to the Reinfords to fill up on water. As I was filling the water tank, I noticed one of the trailer tires looked like a bear had been chewing on it. I did have a spare tire along, so I didn't pay much attention to it. I put over 200 gallons of water in the tank, which in retrospect, would make the trailer weigh well over 1,600 pounds.

After filling the tank, I fired up the Suburban and heard the most awful rattling sounds from the engine, and the oil pressure showed 0. I figured the gauge didn't work, like most everything else on the vehicle, but I decided to check the oil anyway. I knew I was leaving puddles of transmission fluid everywhere, but figured the engine oil was fine. But alas, no oil on the dip stick. Even a fine, reliable vehicle like the Suburban needs oil, so I borrowed the Reinford's Suburban (which looks 50 years newer) and went to town for oil.

After returning, I finally made it out the lane with my Suburban and the water tank. After driving a few miles down the Sterling Highway, I noticed the trailer jerking around like mad, and people behind me swerving around like drunks (I couldn't see the trailer very well because the mirrors didn't stay put). I pulled over, and sure enough, the chewed up tired had flew to pieces. I pulled the jack out, only to discover that somehow this was the same jack the limo had crushed when it tried to kill me earlier in the year. This jack did not work. I had like 4 jacks back at the cabin, but somehow this one was in the vehicle. I made mental notes to throw this jack out so this would not happen again.

Soon, the Reinford's roadside assistance showed up with a spare floor jack. It only took a minute or two to change the tire after that, and I was on the way. I actually got the whole way back to our cabin after this. Driving in our lane, which had frozen up, and was quite bumpy, I noticed the water tank tilting at an odd angle. After pulling up in front of the cabin, I realized that the trailer frame had collapsed. We were all in a hurry to go to Roscoes, as this was now after 6 pm. As everyone was jumping in the suburban, I noticed that now the suburban had a flat tire! No problem, I have a spare. However the spare tire's rim did not clear the hub. As all Alaskans do when the vehicles quit, I decided to just drive the 4 wheeler there instead. So we called our order in to Roscoes, and I left on the 4 wheeler. After all, I thought, Roscoes is only like 5 miles away. (9 miles, if you count the 4 miles down tall tree)

There are these little cool 4 wheeler paths beside the highway. What I didn't realize is that they were made by homicidal maniacs. They went through and over mud bogs, ravines, cliffs, and who knows what else. After driving 12 miles I soon began to realize that Roscoes was further than I thought. No problem, I'll just drive faster. Soon however I found the 4 wheeler way deep in half frozen mud, and it was very stuck. I almost despaired, then realized that hey, I have winch on this thing. I hooked up to a nearby tree, and the winch pulled it out slick as a whistle. This time, however, I decided enough of this stupid trail. I was cold, and very, very wet at this point. I drove down the Sterling Highway at 60 mph, and soon got to Roscoes.

I was nearly frozen, and did not relish the thought of driving back. I had taken over an hour and half to get there, and the temps were below freezing. I must have look pitiful, because one of the Roscoes staff drove me and the pizza back to our place. We enjoyed a late dinner of Pizza and clam chowder around 10:30 that night.

All I can say is "Thank God" for the Reinfords, and "Thank God" I didn't get a ticket for driving around without a license plate on the trailer, and the fact I didn't get a ticket for driving a 4 wheeler several miles down the biggest and only highway in this area. And "Thank God" for that $59 winch special when I bought the four wheeler, otherwise it would have been winch less and stranded. The strange part? I like Alaska even better than ever. All this pain in the neck stuff keeps the riff raff out. Oh, and I think I'll nominate Marlene for a "wife of the year award".

Thanks for reading, Matt

Grizzly Bear Attack! -Chapter 14

A true story from a friend in Alaska that happened on 10/11/2012

One of my friends in Alaska is Gareth Byers (on page 39 he is sitting on the snowmobile trailer), and at the time this happened he farmed over 600 acres. His main operation was dairy. On several occasions he was missing full grown cows, which he eventually found half eaten in the woods. Bears had killed them in his pasture, and hauled them hundreds of yards off into the woods. Naturally when a friend, Bob, asked Gareth if he could go hunt bears on his farm, he said "yes".

Gareth was out of town when Bob went out in the hay field with his .338 rifle to see if he could find any bears. Bob had never shot a brown bear, or "grizzly" as they are call in the interior. He was excited about having a good chance of finally connecting with one. As Bob was sitting in the field, with half an hour of daylight left, he noticed movement behind him. He slowly turned his head, looking over his shoulder, and saw a bear walking towards the woods. Carefully he raised his rifle, as best as he could in that position, and fired. The brown bear bolted towards the woods, and Bob quickly worked the action and fired again. He knew at least one of those shots was a direct hit on the vital area. Excited, he picked up his phone and called his wife. "I got one, a good hit" he told her.

Gareth was still out of town when he got a call from Bob. "I just shot a bear" he said. "Got a good solid hit, but it ran off into the thick brush, I'm going in after it." Gareth, knowing this was a classic hunter gets mauled by bear scenario, suggested he call some other guys to help go in after it, wishing he was there to help. Bob did not want the bear to remain dead in the woods overnight, as there were many other brown bears in the area and they will eat dead bears.

Bob called his son Ethan, and a buddy Daniel, and they both agreed to come out. As they showed up, both carrying .44 magnum revolvers, it was starting to get dark. Bob decided he would park his truck with the headlights and light bar facing into the thick brush. This would allow them to see what was going on. Bob handed Ethan his .338 and carried a .44 mag. With the truck parked, and lights on, guns drawn, they cautiously approached the woods. It was now fully dark. "Normally" explained Bob to me later, "I would have carried a backpack full of ammo, but this was supposed to be a quick game retrieval operation."

Soon they had walked further than they anticipated, and now only had the lights from their flashlights. They found spots of blood here and there, and occasional pools of blood. It seemed the bear was still alive, and they were pushing it. Daniel suggested that they stop and just come back tomorrow and look for the bear. The woods were quiet-perhaps a little to quiet, and they all reported it "felt spooky". Nobody objected to the idea of leaving and coming tomorrow. Having large, angry wounded bears lurking in the dark tends to do that to people.

As they stood around and programmed the location into their phone GPS's Bob heard a "huff" "huff" and a snort. "Here he comes!" he shouted. Suddenly, there was an ear splitting roar and snarl. The woods echoed with a deafening crashing and thundering. Something very big was coming at them very fast. But they couldn't see it very well yet, for a wall of thick brush and darkness loomed ahead. Bob said "the eyes glowed red in his flashlight" and it "had the most awful look you ever seen." Time seemed to stand still. Bob raised his .44 magnum and started firing. Beside him he could hear Daniel blasting away. Ethan raised his rifle, but it wouldn't fire. "What is going on" he though. He tried a second time. Still nothing. Then he realized the safety was still on. With precious time fading fast, he flipped off the safety. Nobody was concerned about accuracy anymore, as the bear was close enough to hit with a rock.

Now the bear was only feet away. Five feet from them it reared up on his hind legs, long claws flashing in the low light, ready to leap on top of the men. At this point, Bob and Daniel emptied their last rounds, and Ethan's .338 barked, now with the safety off. The impact of the three bullets hitting it at once knocked it over backwards. It raked the air, bellowing and roaring with such ferocity only an angry bear can express. It's jaws snapping and clacking meant it was all business. At this point the three men stood, frozen. Their guns were all empty. There was a very angry bear just feet away. The situation was delicate. And the only extra ammo was a .338 bullet in Bob's pocket. In a few seconds they had fired 13 times on the bear.

Suddenly the bear rolled over and got it's feet on the ground, and walked off, as if nothing had happened. Bob explained they were very relieved by that. The men wasted no time heading back to the truck. Ethan and Daniel walked in the front, and Bob walked backwards behind them, facing the direction the bear left. They returned the next day, in daylight, with guns reloaded, and I'm guessing, lots of extra ammo. But it wasn't needed this time around. The bear was found dead, about 40 feet away. It died in an ambush pose. Skinned out, there were 12 bullet holes in the hide. It had been hit 9 times, but the last 3 shots when through both the chest and back, as it stood on it's hind legs in front of them. The hide measured 8 feet long, the front paws measured 8.5 inches across. Bob's first two shots with the rifle were both liver shots, and the bear was mortally wounded from the start of the adventure. But bears can take a long time to die.

The moral of the story? You can't have too much firepower when tracking wounded grizzly bears. I'm personally partial to the .454 casull and .375 H&H cartridges, but I have heard of bears absorbing plenty of those bullets as well. And the .338 and .44 magnum are not slouches. With bears, you just never know. Gareth personally took several bears with the humble 30 -06 cartridge without needing more than 2 shots, and one bear would have only taken one had he been patient. Welcome to rural Alaska, where life is never boring!

Photos & story courtesy of Bob Suder. Used by permission.

Rattlesnakes in the crawl space

Alaska has no snakes, at least not in the wild. I consider this a huge benefit, as I do not like snakes. Give me large bears any day over sadistic hypodermic needles of death slithering through the grass. Our main man in the Pennsylvania office, Ken, used to work in the pest control business when he lived in Arizona (he was even the town dog catcher for a short time). He has some stories that make my hair stand on end. Here is my favorite:

A customer called in and complained he had a nest of rattlesnakes under his trailer. So Ken responded with his normal array of equipment, plus a semi automatic .22 pistol he had just acquired. Before he used a revolver. Loaded with birdshot, these guns were effective and did not tear large holes in surrounding objects. Ken crawled under the darkness of the trailer with a flashlight and the new pistol. Soon he found his first snake straight ahead of him. One "pop!" and this snake was history. Lurking in the blackness behind the first snake he shot, emerged a second rattlesnake, and Ken now had a problem. His gun had jammed on the first shot. Squeezed into the dark, musty space under the trailer, he couldn't move fast, and this snake was now crawling directly at him.

Ken beat the ground and yelled, waving his bright flash light in the snakes face. Ken confirmed that rattlesnakes eyes glow red. The snake stopped, then retreated back a few moments. This gave Ken enough time to get out of there and reload. He then found several more snakes under the trailer. My recommendation to the homeowner would have been to slide gasoline soaked tires in the crawl space and light up the whole nest. Ken did say "he was a mess for a few days after that". Another time Ken and his family were out boating, and rattlesnakes were swimming past, and trying to board their boat. They beat them back with oars. No wonder they don't live in Arizona anymore...

(right) Ken holding a rattlesnake (below) Patrina, who also works for us, is in the middle. (pictures were taken late 80's)

Suburban breaks down within walking distance of cheap van for sale

Submitted on Sat, 11/08/2014 - 1:01pm

I have a theory that "you can never find a cheap vehicle when you need one", thus you need to buy cheap vehicles whenever you see them for sale. This allows you to have a few handy spares. However this week that theory was shot full of holes (or at least proven to have a few exceptions). I was pulling out of Tall Tree Avenue onto the Sterling Highway when Shane commented "the suburban is really smoking." I replied "I didn't think it was smoking more than normal" and we headed down the road. Soon however, it became obvious the Suburban was suffering a more severe bout of dementia than normal. As it was wheezing and gasping, we passed an old van with a "For Sale" sign in the windshield. Suspecting the Suburban's condition was terminal, I pulled over to the side of the road (It wouldn't accelerate anymore anyway, we were just coasting).

After we stopped, I got out and looked under the Suburban. It was shooting small geysers of transmission fluid in several directions, some of which hit the exhaust and smoked vigorously. "Looks like we'll need to walk" I told Shane, and we started walking back towards the direction of Tall Tree. It was a nice day, and it is always good to get exercise. And, unlike our last breakdown when we had to walk, I had my .454 revolver with, so there was little chance of getting eaten (unlike Pa, you don't need a license to conceal carry handguns, although the .454 is so big it's like hiding a shovel under your coat).

We walked only a hundred yards or so, we came to the old van for sale. It was a 1984 Dodge van, with "$800 or best offer" written on it. I called the number and offered the fellow selling it $500. "Sure, if you take it today" was his response. I replied "I was indeed hoping to drive it away today." So Mike, the guy selling the van, came down from his house to talk to us. (It was parked at the end of his lane)

"Where is your vehicle?" Mike asked. I pointed down the road, and said it broke down, and "we were in the market for another one." So Mike took me on a short drive to an ATM in Anchor Point, I got cash out (the ATM withdraw limit was $400 but I had $95 in my wallet, and he agree to trust me to get him the remaining $5 later) After a quick call to State Farm to get insurance, we were on our way again. I held my breath on the drive to Homer, (well not the entire way) because it didn't have current plates on. However, all went well and we stopped at the DMV, which was on the way to Spenards Lumber anyway. (Alaska, unlike the tyrant DMV's in Pa, lets you transfer titles without dragging the seller along) I was getting lumber to build a shed (no permits needed in Alaska for building things either).

Normally I wouldn't pick old Dodge vans, being a Ford and Chevy fan (yes you can be a fan of both) however the price was right, and as a bonus it had a 4 speed on the floor manual shift. With it's 318 V-8 engine, you can actually burn rubber with it. It is also equipped with a nice hitch.

Ironically the old van must have come from Pennsylvania at one point, because it had some sappy Penn State stickers on the back. No, the van doesn't have a current inspection sticker, and it never will, as they are not needed in Alaska. (notice a pattern here between Alaska and Pa?)

Oh, and this Mike guy? Turns out he is a Suburban guru, with many old Suburban's parked out behind his house. Part of his Suburban collection is one lifted high enough to have what looks like Farmall tractor tires on it. He also has a cheap transmission for sale that will fit right in the Suburban. So I guess the Suburban story is not as finished as I thought it was.

The moral of the story? Always keep $500 cash in your wallet.

Matt

"The Grid" is officially a dinosaur (and an expensive one)

Submitted on Thu, 10/30/2014 - 12:15pm

A few years ago I played around with making hydrogen out of water, and trying to boost fuel mileage with a setup like that. I did manage to go from 18 mpg to 21 mpg with my Ford F350, however the results ranged wildly every tank. You can read articles online about people trying to run generators on water, etc, and they claim the government shuts them down. I suspect most if not all of those folks were just trying to blame their failures to produce electric on the government. One reason I suspect those water conspiracy folks don't have a leg to stand on is this fact: I am producing free electric, and no men in black suits are hiding in the bushes. In fact, many people are producing free electric, and it's easier than ever before. The secret device? Why solar panels, of course.

Yesterday I got my 4 panels online to work with the 2 panels already mounted on the cabin. In overcast conditions they were cranking 60 amps at 12 volts into the battery bank. A few hours of serious charging like that and the batteries are maxed out.

As soon as you mention solar panels, naysayers will blow and trumpet a line of catch phrases like "they don't last more than 5 years", "the sun doesn't always shine", "you never get your money back from those things", etc, etc. These tiresome sayings were true a few years ago, but prices have dropped considerably and panels have gotten much better in quality. True, the sun still doesn't shine all the time, but the trick is to buy enough panels to charge a thing called "batteries" so you can use electric when the sun goes down. I have a small battery bank, 8 230 am hour batteries, and they provide more than enough electric over night. In fact we can do wash, brew coffee and run the fridge all at once without the system melting down. Also, the batteries I am using are just garden variety 6 volt golf cart batteries. There are even more serious batteries that would do even better.

People ask "when will electric lines get run to your place?", and my answer is "never, I hope". Just as rats followed the ships in the old days, the 'rats follow the electric lines. The math does hold out- solar panels are the way to go.

A disclaimer is needed here: I am not a tree hugger. If burning a stack of tires made free electric, I might be doing that. Not having huge clouds of black smoke over your property is a positive thing though. It would also pose a forest fire threat in the summer.

Note: as much trouble as I have with gas powered generators, I would hate the thought of keeping a "water powered" combustion generator working.

I hope your not shocked, Matt

Our neighbor Ron told us that it "always snows a few inches around Halloween." Sure enough, we got some snow right over that time. I think it may have been that exact day, but I didn't write it down and don't quite remember. It was hardly any snow for Alaskan standards, but I couldn't help but try out the "snow machine".

The snow machine worked well running over the frozen muskeg, because while there was hardly enough snow, the frozen grass underneath helped cushion it. I was delighted to find I could punch the throttle and bring the front skis off the ground, very easily. Once or twice I flipped the machine while making turns. It takes some getting used to. The children all enjoyed rides, and even Marlene took a turn running it.

The four wheelers were also a lot of fun to run in the snow. I'm sure this would be a different case if you had several feet of snow. But with just a few inches, they blew right through it. Sometime I will need to build a garage of some sort. I found changing oil in the "wheelers" got tiresome outside in the snow. A typically winter around here will have two feet of snow on the ground in January, according to the neighbors.

As is typical of Marlin, when they dropped of their van it had a full tank of gas. Eventually we needed to put more gas in it. So I stopped in at the local gas station in Ninilchik, and topped it off. Jumping into the van to leave, it started, sputtered, then stopped. I tried again. It would crank, but not even try to start. This was puzzling, from what people tell me, newer vehicles never break down. I called Marlin and asked if he had any suggestions. Marlin was out delivering sheds, and could pick us up, but not for a few hours.

Not knowing what to do, I suggested walking back to our cabin and getting the 2 seater van (our "good" van was still in the garage). But that was over 17 miles away, and would take a good deal of time. Finally I called Alan. Surprisingly, Alan didn't hang up on me (he has never hung up on me, I just thought he might since I am constantly bothering him).

It was decided that Twila, Alan's wife, would come down and give us a ride back to the cabin. The gas station was across the street from Roscoe's Pizza, so we headed over there to eat, while waiting on Twila (they were about a 40 minute drive away). After about 45 minutes, Twila, bless her heart, came walking in. We insisted she eat some pizza before we leave, as a very small token of appreciation. Before we left, someone suggested we try starting the van up again.

Thinking it would be a waste of time, I walked over and tried the van. It started right up, and purred flawlessly. Later, I discovered that the first time you start it after refueling you need to hold the gas down to keep it running. After you reach 45 mph then it starts working right until you fill the tank up again. I called the Chevy dealer and asked them about this, and they acted like I was talking about poltergeists. The salesman commented he had never heard of such a problem before. Talking to them was a waste of time, so we just used the van like that. It felt good to know I wasn't the only one who owned vehicles that seemed to have a mind of their own. We were very thankful for the use of the van, even if it did strange things.

Soon the garage had our van finished, and it was good to have it back. I must also say I'm very impressed with Jasper transmissions. Sure, we had trouble with it, but they covered the cost of replacing it. It's not if a company makes a mistake, but how they deal with it that impresses me. I plan to use Jasper for any replacement engines or transmissions in the future. We returned Marlin's van, and started to gain a sense of independence.

The ultimate ATV accessory - works for hauling tires, water, groceries and children

Submitted on Fri, 11/28/2014 - 9:55am

When outfitting your ATV, there are many options to consider. Winches, oversized tires, gun racks, snorkel kits, etc. While those are fine things, the feature I found most useful with my 4 wheeler was a 140 quart Igloo ice chest. Like most great inventions, I discovered this by accident. The fateful night that I drove the Kymco to Ninilchick for pizza, I strapped the ice chest on the 4 wheeler.

A quick note on town names: Alaska has the best town names of any state. Just down the road from us is "Ninilchick", and "Kasilof". There is also "Soldotna", "Kalifornsky", "Nikiski", "Kenai", "Clam Gulch" and of course "Anchor Point", not as exotic sounding but still sturdy names that have a neat ring. Compared to "Blue Ball", "Intercourse", "Virginville" and "Bird-in-Hand" of Lancaster County, Pa, they sound downright incredible. In fact, it sounds like perverts were naming the towns in Pa. (of course, perhaps the town names in Alaska mean bad things in Russian, I don't know)

Back to the ice chest on the 4 wheeler. Of course, one problem with hauling pizza in an ice chest is that it doesn't fit, without being cut in half.(the pizza) But I figured that would be better than cold pizza. After I eventually got the 4 wheeler back to the cabin, I discovered many other uses for this ice chest. It came in handy for hauling groceries, tires, water and even children. (although in Pa you would probably get locked up for hauling children in an ice chest) Note: leave the lid off or open.

One possible problem is that your ice chest will get more wear and tear than if you just stocked cold drinks in it. Given the fact most folks don't care about the resell value of their ice chest, this shouldn't be a problem. So go ahead, give it a shot!

Matt

Samantha and Mary Kate sit on the sofa. Sometimes they pretend to act bored in the cabin. They did enjoy playing in the snow, but would get the floor all wet when it was time to come in. Eventually we will build a front porch.

Our multi purpose ice chest in action. The 7 gallon water containers fit perfectly inside it! I could easily haul 21 gallons without any problems.

Above is sunset over our muskeg. Below: The location we hope to build a "real house", after which the cabin will be guest quarters.

One tiresome part about living in Alaska, is that you need to travel 4,000 miles to family get togethers. That is until you convince your in-laws and extended family to move to Alaska, which so far has been unfruitful. Our extended family had not yet moved to Alaska, and everyone wanted to see us for the holidays. The fact this also overlapped with Pennsylvania's deer season was perhaps, a coincidence.

The trip from Alaska to Pennsylvania seemed shorter every time we took it. Most folks seemed amazed that we drive back and forth so much. This time, our trip to Pennsylvania only took 4.5 days, beating our earlier 5.5 day record. We pulled this off by driving straight thru, stopping only one night somewhere to sleep. Of course we did sleep other than this, we took turns sleeping while the other person drove.

On our way south through the interior of Canada, we hit temperatures in the –20 degrees Fahrenheit for hundreds of miles. Because of this, we only shut the van down once, when we stopped at a motel for the night. The rest of the time it ran 'round the clock.

I get a kick out of the Canadian road signs, like the one above. Does this mean to be on the lookout for suicidal truck drivers ramming brick walls? Below: We saw quite a few reindeer while driving the Alcan.

Pennsylvania was kind to me in their 2014 deer season. I harvested an 8 point buck and a small antlerless deer, it was actually a button buck. These were both taken with a 12 gauge slug gun, purchased several years ago from Beavertown Guns & Grocery. It felt odd getting a non resident hunting license.

A Lane is Born-Chapter 15

Late December Alan Reinford, Dan Zimmerman, and even the neighbor Ron pitched in, finishing the lane. The original plans were to finish the lane earlier, but it wouldn't get cold enough to freeze up our dirt road before that. The stone was to be hauled from Ron's gravel pit, and had we done it before freeze up it would have torn up his driveway and the road. It was a lot of hauling, 1,980 yards of gravel hauled.

No more floundering around in the mud trying to get to the cabin, or packing the children out on four wheelers to go to church. We do enjoy the new lane!

Tour of Anchor Point, Alaska

Anchor Point is the closest town to our property. Captain Cook lost his anchor here on his famous arctic expedition of 1778-1779, or so the legend goes. I like to think he walked 4 miles inland, sat down where my land is, and buried some gold (although I have not found any). This town does have some interesting shops and things to see. Anchor Point is located about a 15 minute drive north of Homer, and a 50 minute drive south of Soldotna.

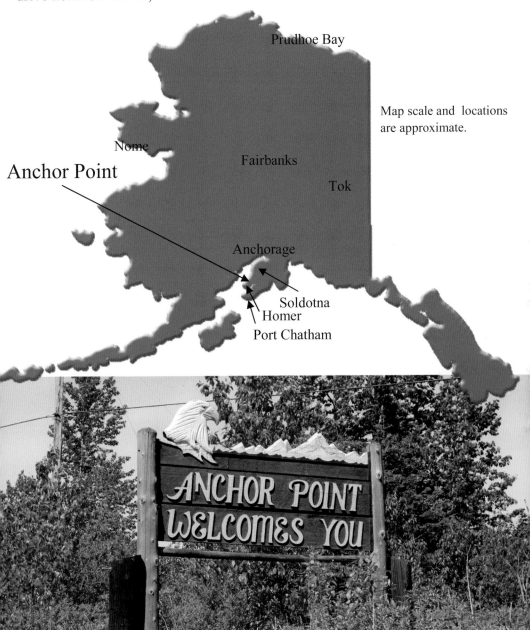

Prudhoe Bay

Map scale and locations are approximate.

Nome

Fairbanks

Tok

Anchor Point

Anchorage

Soldotna

Homer

Port Chatham

You want to go west? Here is the place to be! Below is the spring where we get our drinking water, located on the outskirts of Anchor Point.

How many laundromats do you know of that also have a tanning booths, soft serve ice cream, showers, a deli and serve expresso? Welcome to "The Cheeky Moose"!

Would you like to dine in a bus? You have come to the right place! Not sure if this bus still has a valid registration or insurance.

We do have a small hardware store in town. I was impressed with their prices, they are very competitive.

Anchor Point has not one bus restaurant, but two! This is "Ramiro's" a Mexican restaurant. Sorry no eating in the bus-take out only here.

Alaskans are big on several things, including coffee and fishing. As mentioned before, even the laundromat serves expresso. There are several stores in town selling fishing tackle as well. Big time coffee shops, such as Starbucks, are few and far between but small coffee shops are everywhere (on the Kenai Peninsula). Even the local tire shop sells coffee and expresso. And the reason for the fishing should be obvious, there are many world class places to fish within a few miles.

The Anchor River, for example is within the town limits. This river is crowded the opening days of the various salmon runs. You need to read the fishing laws carefully though. Some parts of the river are closed while others are open, and the seasons can open or close at a moments notice with emergency orders from Alaska Fish & Game. Alaska State Troopers also enforce the game laws, and there is a State Trooper office right in Anchor Point. My one neighbor (who I have not named anywhere in the book) reported poaching a moose "because his wife told him to." The result? Every month for a year he had to go to a court hearing dealing with it. "I'm never doing that again" he said.

Alaska might not have many rules-but don't break the ones they do have, especially the fish and game rules. You can drive a car without a vehicle inspection, build a house without a permit, carry your handgun without a permit-but don't shoot a moose without a license!

The Anchor River has many splendid fishing opportunities, including King Salmon, Sockeye, Steelheads, and the list goes on and on. There is even gold in the river! (no fishing license needed to look for that)

"Last Frontier Trading Post" has a little bit of everything. I have seen boats, 4 wheelers, Elvis memorabilia, fishing lures and many other types of items. It's a must visit for genuine Alaskan gifts and oddities. Not full of plastic touristy junk.

Above: Sunset over Cook Inlet.   Below: Mountains and lake near Denali National Park. Photos by Josh Snader